Battles Royal of the Chessboard

Collected and presented by
R. N. Coles

Cadogan Books
London

This edition published 1995 by Cadogan Books plc, London House,
Parkgate Road, London, SW11 4NQ

ISBN 1 85744 182 6

Printed and bound in Finland by Werner Söderström Oy

CONTENTS

PAGE

INTRODUCTION ix

GAMES :—

* *An asterisk signifies the winner. No asterisk signifies a drawn game.*

1. McDonnell—*de Labourdonnais, 47th match game, London, 1834 11
King's Bishop's Opening
2. *de Labourdonnais—McDonnell, 78th match game, London, 1834 14
Queen's Gambit
3. Boncourt—*Saint-Amant, Paris, 1839 18
Giuoco Piano
4. Staunton—Saint-Amant, 2nd match game, London, 1843 20
King's Bishop's Opening
5. *Bird—Horwitz, London tournament, 1851 .. 23
Ruy Lopez
6. von der Lasa—*Staunton, 2nd match game, Brussels, 1853 26
King's Bishop's Opening
7. Anderssen—Morphy, 2nd match game, Paris, 1858 28
Ruy Lopez
8. Anderssen—*Steinitz, 3rd match game, London, 1866 31
Evans Gambit
9. Zukertort—*Steinitz, 1st match game, London, 1872 34
Giuoco Piano
10. Mason—*Zukertort, London tournament, 1883 .. 37
Queen's Gambit Declined
11. Burn—*Mackenzie, 4th match game, London, 1886 41
Queen's Pawn Game
12. *Tarrasch—Gunsberg, Frankfort tournament, 1887 44
French Defence
13. *Mackenzie—Blackburne, Bradford tournament, 1888 46
Queen's Pawn Game
14. Weiss—Tchigorin, 1st tie-match game, New York tournament, 1889 49
Ruy Lopez
15. *Pillsbury—Tarrasch, Hastings tournament, 1895 52
Pillsbury Attack
16. *Steinitz—Pillsbury, St. Petersburg tournament, 1896 54
Petroff Defence
17. Pillsbury—Tchigorin, St. Petersburg tournament, 1896 57
Tchigorin Defence

18. Charousek—Pillsbury, Nuremburg tournament, 1896 60
Falkbeer Counter-Gambit
19. Steinitz—Lasker, 5th match game, Moscow, 1896 .. 63
Pillsbury Attack
20. Lasker—*Blackburne, London tournament, 1899 65
Ruy Lopez
21. Janowski—Burn, Paris tournament, 1900 .. 67
Ruy Lopez
22. *Marshall—Marco, Monte Carlo tournament, 1904 70
Scotch Gambit
23. *Lasker—Napier, Cambridge Springs tournament, 1904 75
Sicilian Defence
24. *Duras—Teichmann, Ostend tournament, 1906 .. 78
Ruy Lopez
25. *Rubinstein—Lasker, St. Petersburg tournament, 1909 81
Tarrasch Defence
26. Marshall—*Capablanca, 11th match game, New York, 1909 84
Pillsbury Attack
27. Schlechter—Lasker, 7th match game, Berlin, 1910 87
Sicilian Defence
28. Mieses—*Capablanca, Exhibition game, Berlin 1913 90
Centre Game
29. *Capablanca—Marshall, New York tournament, 1918 93
Ruy Lopez
30. Rubinstein—*Alekhine, London tournament, 1922 95
Slav Defence
31. *Reti—Becker, Vienna tournament, 1923 98
Reti System
32. Znosko-Borovsky—Alekhine, Paris tournament, 1925 100
Alekhine Defence
33. *Tartakower—Bogolyubov, London tournament, 1927 102
Ponziani Opening
34. Alekhine—Capablanca, 22nd match game, Buenos Aires, 1927 105
Pillsbury Attack
35. Capablanca—Nimzowitch, Kissingen tournament, 1928 109
Nimzo-Indian Defence
36. Euwe—Bogolyubov, 8th match game, 1928 .. 112
Pillsbury Attack
37. *Vidmar—Euwe, Carlsbad tournament, 1929 .. 114
Queen's Pawn Game
38. Alekhine—Bogolyubov, 11th match game, Weisbaden, 1929 116
Pillsbury Attack
39. Spielmann—*Stoltz, Bled tournament, 1931 .. 120
Queen's Gambit

CONTENTS

40. COLLE—*KASHDAN, Bled tournament, 1931 .. 123
Colle System

41. STOLTZ—*COLLE, Bled tournament, 1931 126
Alekhine Defence

42. EUWE—YATES, Hastings tournament, 1932 128
King's Indian Defence

43. SULTAN KHAN—*ALEKHINE, Folkestone team tournament, 1933 131
Queen's Pawn Game

44. SPIELMANN—LASKER, Moscow tournament, 1935 .. 136
Scotch Game

45. EUWE—ALEKHINE, 19th match game, Eindhoven, 1937 138
Nimzo-Indian Defence

46. RESHEVSKY—BOTVINNIK, Avro tournament, 1938 .. 141
Nimzo-Indian Defence

47. EUWE—KERES, Avro tournament, 1938 143
Dutch Defence

48. FINE—*KERES, Avro tournament, 1938 145
Ruy Lopez

49. *BOTVINNIK — ALEXANDER, Anglo-Russian radio match, 1946 149
Nimzo-Indian Defence

50. SMYSLOV—KATETOV, Moscow-Prague match, 1946 .. 152
French Defence

INDEX OF OPENINGS 155

INTRODUCTION

I can do no better in giving my reasons for making the present collection of games than to tell the story of an incident which occurred at a British Chess Federation congress. Two moderate players were engaged in a very complicated and exciting game and a well-known master was looking on. When the game finished in a draw White said to Black, " I enjoyed that. It was a really good game." " Good ? " interposed the master. " But White could have won a piece nine moves ago, and Black three moves later missed a forced mate in six ! " The pieces were set up again and the correctness of the master's analysis was established. " All the same it was a rattling good game," said White. A look of puzzled exasperation came over the master's face. " The mate in six, with a queen sacrifice and a knight sacrifice, that is good, yes, but you did not see it." " No," said Black, " and I never shall see things like that though I study master brilliancies till the cows come home." " Then the game is not good ? " " All right," agreed Black, " it was not good, but it was the most enjoyable game I've had for months." With a helpless shrug of his expressive shoulders the master left them.

The artist is a being apart, searching ever after perfection ; the rest of us can admire works of art but we cannot create them. As with art, so with chess, the difference being that we do not leave the playing of the game to the experts ; we continue to extract the utmost pleasure from the humble rough-and-tumble chess of which we are capable, and if we occasionally miss a brilliancy because our imagination will not rise to it we probably get greater pleasure from a greater number of games than the artist does who cannot appreciate anything less than perfection. So long as a game is hard fought, and especially if it is complicated and exciting, that game is enjoyable and good enough for most of us.

Many collections of games have been made in which the brilliancies which are beyond the average player are beautifully displayed. We admire them but cannot relate them to our own play over the board. We watch the defeated master in the ineluctable toils, but our own opponents wriggle out of our best laid schemes and as like as not we then have to struggle to avoid defeat ourselves ; we seek to attain supremacy only to find our opponent securing the ascendancy on some other part of the board. This is chess as we know it and as we have to play it.

The present collection consists of master examples of the sort of game which White and Black enjoyed so much at the congress ; here may be seen how the masters react when a combination goes wrong or when their opponents fight back ; in these games neither player is content to be smothered by the brilliant imagination of the other, nor to allow master technique to win a won game by copybook methods ; here is complicated, fighting chess.

A few of the games will be old favourites, which could not well be omitted from a collection of this nature ; such are Nos. 15 and 20, but if their presence serves to whet the appetite for more like them, well and good. Many of the others will be less well known. The notes are indebted to many sources for analyses, and these have frequently passed through so many hands that it has not been possible to acknowledge the original except in a few cases ; the few original notes are designed to throw into relief the up-and-down nature of the various battles. As for the title—the contestants are all of the blood royal of chess aristocracy and the games are in all senses Battles Royal.

R.N.C.
Harrow, 1948

L. C. M. de Labourdonnais (1795–1840) was the greatest chess-master of the first half of the nineteenth century, no rival worthy of him being found until 1834, when he came to London and played A. McDonnell (1798–1835) in a series of games which still bears comparison with those of any later age. The Frenchman won the majority because of his greater versatility and position judgment. The premature death of both players was an irreparable loss and it is fitting that they lie now in adjacent graves at Kensal Green.

GAME 1

MCDONNELL-DE LABOURDONNAIS

1st game of the 4th match and 47th of the series.
London, 1834.

KING'S BISHOP'S OPENING

1. P—K4 P—K4
2. B—B4 B—B4
3. P—QB3

Q—Kt4 was a later fashion.

3. Q—K2
4. Kt—B3 P—Q3
5. O—O B—Kt3
6. P—Q4 Kt—KB3
7. Kt—R3 B—Kt5

If Kt×P; 8 R—K1, P—KB4; 9 B—Q5.

8. Kt—B2 QKt—Q2

And now if Kt×P; 9 B—Q5, at once.

9. Q—Q3

Better was B—KKt5. Black is now able to take advantage of the queen's position with a beautiful pawn sacrifice which opens a phase of absorbing interest and complexity.

9. P—Q4
10. KP×P

An alternative was B×P, but not QP×P, P×B; 11 P×Kt, P×Q; 12 P×Q, P×Kt; winning a piece. Even now White must play with the greatest exactness to avoid losing a piece.

10. P—K5
11. Q—Q2 P×Kt
12. R—K1 Kt—K5
13. Q—B4 P—KB4
14. P×P

[Diagram 1]

14. P—Kt4
15. Q—K3

If Q×KtP, not 15 . . ., Kt×Q; 16 R×Qch., K×R; 17

(BLACK) DE LABOURDONNAIS

(WHITE) MCDONNELL

Position before Black's 14th move.

(DIAGRAM 1)

B×Ktch., and 18 P×B with two pieces for the rook, but 15 . . ., Q×Q; 16 B×Q, B×BP; with advantage to Black.

15. Kt—K4

A fine continuation threatening both Kt×B and Kt×Pch.

16. B—Kt5ch.

This holds the extra pawn, but B—K2 was probably sounder.

16. P—B3
17. P×B

Not 17 P×P, Kt×Pch.; retaining the piece.

17. Kt×KtP

Black must proceed with care. If P×B; 18 P×P, winning back one of the knights with the better game.

18. Q—K2 P×B
19. P—B3

Now it is White who must be careful. If at once 19 Q×Pch., K—B1; 20 P—B3, Kt—Q3; 21 Q—B1, Kt—K4; 22 P—B4, P×P; 23 B×P, Q—Kt2ch., and 24 . . ., Kt (K)—B2; retaining the piece.

19. Kt (Kt)—B3
20. P×Kt Kt×KP
21. Q×Pch. Q—Q2
22. Q×Qch. K×Q
23. P—B4

A new phase begins, each player endeavouring to use the passed pawns.

23. QR—K1
24. P—B5 B—Q1
25. P—Q6

Better was B—K3. Now the bishop cannot cross to the defence of the king.

25. P—B5
26. P—Kt4 KR—B1
27. R—B1

Black's P—Kt5 cannot be long prevented, but the rook will be needed here whether it is or not.

27. P—KR4
28. Kt—R3 B—B3
29. B—Kt2 P—Kt5
30. Kt—B4

Not 30 R×P, B×Pch.

30. P—B6
31. Kt—K5ch. B×Kt
32. P×B P—R5
33. QR—Q1 P—B7ch.
34. K—R1 P—R6

Now 35 . . ., P—Kt6 ; is a serious threat, after which White has to avoid both 36 . . ., P—Kt7 Mate and 36 P×P, Kt ×Pch. ; with Black winning the exchange.

35. R—Q3 R—KKt1
36. P—Kt5 P—Kt6

(BLACK) DE LABOURDONNAIS

(WHITE) MCDONNELL

Position before White's 37th move

(DIAGRAM 2)

37. P×P R×KtP

Stronger than Kt×Pch. ; 38 R×Kt, R×R ; 39 R×P, and White's pawns compensate for the loss of the exchange. Clearly the rook cannot be taken.

38. R—Q4 R (K)—KKt1

White's last move has brought Black's attack to a standstill. Insufficient would be 38 . . ., R×P ; 39 P—B6ch., P×P ; 40 P×Pch., K×P ; 41 R—B4ch., R—B4 ; 42 R×Kt, while 38 . . ., R—Kt8ch. ; leads to no more than a draw after 39 R×R, Kt—Kt6ch. ; 40 K—R2, P×R=Qch. ; 41 K×Q, Kt—K7ch. ; 42 K—R2, Kt×R ; 43 B×Kt, and the pawns will be too strong ; for example, 43 . . ., K—K3 (or R—KKt1 ; 44 P—B6ch., P×P ; 45 P×Pch., K×P ; 46 B×P, R—Kt7ch. ; 47 K×P, R×P) ; 44 P—B6, P—Kt3 ; 45 P—Q7, R—KKt1 ; 46 K×P.

39. P—K6ch.

To prevent a Black rook going to KR1.

39. K—Q1

Not K×P ; 40 R×Ktch., K—Q4 ; 41 R—K5ch., K—B5 ; 42 R×P, and Black's last hope of attack is broken.

40. R (4)—Q1

In spite of the threat on KKt1, White can play R×Kt for then 40 . . ., R—Kt8ch. ; 41 K—R2, R×R (threatening R—R8ch.) ; 42 B—B6ch., K—B1 ; 43 P—Q7ch., K—B2 ; 44 P—Q8=Qch., R×Q ; 45 B×Rch., K×B ; 46 R—KB4, but he hopes now for more.

40. P—R7

Threatening to win by 41 . . ., R—Kt8ch. ; 42 K×P, R (1)—Kt7ch. ; 43 K—R3, Kt—Kt4ch. ; 44 K—R4, R—R7 Mate. If White replies 41 K×P, then the combination of R(6)—Kt3 with the mating threat forces White to play his pawns as in the actual game.

41. P—K7ch. K—Q2
42. P—B6ch. P×P
43. P×Pch. K×P
44. P—K8=Qch. R×Q
45. K×P

Sooner or later he must take the pawn. If 45 P—Q7, R (K)—KKt1; 46 P—Q8=Q, R×Q; 47 R×R, R—Kt8ch.; 48 K×P, R×R; 49 R—KB8, K—Q4; and wins. However, Black's reply to the text move also decides the game.

45. R—K3
46. R—B1ch. K—Kt4

More decisive than K×P; 47 KR—Q1ch., K—K2; 48 R—B7ch., K—K1; 49 B—Kt7, R (K)—KKt3; 50 R—QKt1, K—Q1; etc. It is the virtual end of a very great struggle.

47. P—R4ch. K—Kt5
48. B—B3ch. R×B
49. R×R K×R
50. P—Q7 R—Q3
51. K—Kt2 R×P
52. R—B1ch. K—Q6
53. K—B1 K—K6
Resigns.

GAME 2

DE LABOURDONNAIS-MCDONNELL

2nd game of the 6th match and 78th of the series.
London, 1834.

QUEEN'S GAMBIT

1. P—Q4 P—Q4
2. P—QB4 P×P
3. P—K4 P—K4
4. P—Q5 P—KB4
5. Kt—QB3 Kt—KB3
6. B×P B—B4
7. Kt—B3 P×P

A very famous game, the 50th of the series, continued 7 . . ., Q—K2; 8 B—Kt5, B×Pch.; 9 K—B1, B—Kt3; 10 Q—K2, P—B5; 11 R—Q1, B—Kt5; 12 P—Q6, P×P; 13 Kt—Q5, Kt×Kt; 14 B×Q, Kt—K6ch.; and Black won magnificently.

8. Kt—KKt5 O—O

Daring, for after 9 P—Q6 dis. ch., K—R1; 10 Kt—B7ch., R×Kt; 11 B×R, Black has nothing better than P×P, though his pressure in the centre is then considerable.

9. O—O B—Q3
10. Kt—K6

Kt(5)×KP leads to an equal game. White finds that a pawn on K6 exerts less pressure than one on Q5.

10. B×Kt
11. P×B K—R1
12. B—KKt5 Kt—B3
13. Kt×P Q—K2
14. K—R1 QR—Q1
15. Q—R4 P—QR3
16. B—Q5 Kt—Q5

Sacrificing a pawn on the Q side in order to force White to give up his KP. The threat is 17 . . ., P—B3; 18 B—Kt3, P—Kt4; 19 Q×RP, R—R1; 20 Q—Kt6, KR—QKt1; winning the queen.

17. B×Kt P×B
18. B×P Q×P
19. QR—K1

Reluctant to accept the offer. If 19 Q×P, P—KB4; 20 Kt×B, R×Kt; 21 Q—R4 (not Q—R3, Kt—B7; nor Q—Q3, P—K5), P—K5; with a strong position.

19. P—KB4
20. Kt—B3

Threatening Q×Kt.

20. Q—B3
21. Q×P

Better was R—K3, for the attack on his king is stronger than is at first apparent.

21. P—K5
22. Q—B4

Now R—K3 was essential.

(BLACK) MCDONNELL

(WHITE) DE LABOURDONNAIS

Position before Black's 22nd move.

(DIAGRAM 3)

22. B×P

Clever but not best. After Kt—B6; 23 R—K3 (P×Kt, Q—K4), Q—R5; White is lost.

23. R—K3

Not 23 K×B, Q—R5ch.; 24 K—Kt1, Kt—B6ch.; 25 P×Kt, R—Kt1ch.; and mates. With the text move White begins to fight his way out.

23. Kt—B6

The only move to continue the attack, but better was B—Q3.

24. R×Kt P×R
25. K×B R—Q5
26. Q—B5 P×P

He cannot prevent the bishop returning to the defence of the king, for Q or R—R5ch.; 27 K—Kt1, R—Kt1; 28 B×P, with a solid position.

27. B×P R—KKt1

Threatening 28 . . ., R—R5ch.; 29 K—Kt1 (B—R3, R×Bch.; and mates), Q—Kt2; 30 Q—Q5, R—K5; winning.

28. P—B4

This loses the pawn. Better was B—R3, and if R—R5; 29 Q—K3.

28. Q—Kt2
29. R—B2 R×P
30. R—K2 R—KKt5
31. B—R3 R—KB5
32. R—Kt2

If Q—K3 (to prevent the

threatened checks on Kt1 and Kt3), Q—Q5 would lead to positions similar to those in the text.

32. Q—Q5
33. Q×Qch. R×Q
34. R—KB2

After 34 B×P, R×Rch.; 35 K×R, R—Q7ch.; White could not hope to win.

34. P—B5
35. P—R4 K—Kt2
36. B—Kt2

Envisaging the advance and possible queening of the QRP. Black's reply prepares a subtle counter to this plan.

36. R—KB1
37. P—R5 R—Q3
38. B—Kt7 R—B4
39. P—R6 P—B6

(BLACK) MCDONNELL

(WHITE) DE LABOURDONNAIS

Position before White's 40th move.

(DIAGRAM 4)

By this sudden counter-attack (threatening R—KKt3 and R—R4 Mate, and later another mate on KR8) Black hopes to force 40 B×P, R×P; ending the threat on the QR file, but he is one move too late.

40. K—Kt1 R—Kt3ch.
41. K—B1 R—R3
42. K—K1 R—R8ch.
43. K—Q2 R—R8

Now Black seems to have succeeded in his plan to halt the QRP, and is in a position to advance his own pawns.

44. K—Q3

This unassuming move is a necessary preparation for yet another plan to advance the QRP.

44. K—B3

Hoping to induce White to waste time capturing the QBP while he mobilises his K side. Both players are still scheming to win.

45. Kt—Q5ch.

Apparently accepting the bait, but actually continuing the plan made the previous move to bring the knight to QR3 or QR5, cutting off the Black rook.

45. K—Kt4
46. Kt—K3 R—B3

The purpose of White's 44th move is now clear; Kt—B4 cannot be prevented, whereas if only 47 Kt—B2 had been available, Black could have replied 47 . . ., R(8)—R4 or R5.

47. Kt—B4 P—R4

If R—R5; 48 P—Kt3, R—R8 (more point to White's 44th; with the K on Q2, Black could now play R—R7ch.); 49 P—Kt4, R—R5 (aiming to get rid of both White's Q-side pawns for his rook); 50 K—B3, and only then Kt—R5. Black therefore proceeds with his own plans, though he stood a better chance of drawing by R×P; 48 B×R, R×B; 49 R×P, P—R4.

48. Kt—R3 R—Q8ch.
49. K—B2 R—Q1
50. P—R7 K—Kt5
51. P—R8=Q R×Q
52. B×R

White is now two pieces ahead but Black's pawns are becoming increasingly dangerous.

52. K—Kt6
53. R—B1 K—Kt7
54. R—Q1 P—B3

Cutting off the bishop and threatening P—B7. White is now in difficulties and his next move suggests that the best plan he can find is to play B—B8 and then sacrifice the bishop for the RP, with a draw.

55. B—Kt7 P—B7
56. Kt—B4 R—K3

Not P—B8=Q; 57 Kt—K3ch.

57. Kt—Q2 P—R5
58. P—Kt4

Finding the correct method just in time, which is to reopen the diagonal.

58. P—R6
59. P—Kt5 P—R7
60. B×Pch. K—Kt6
61. B—R1 R—QKt3
62. R—Kt1 R—Kt1
63. P—Kt6 Resigns.

For after 64 Kt—B1ch., K—R6; 65 R—Kt3ch., the pawns begin to fall.

P. C. F. de Saint-Amant (1800–1873) became the leader of French chess after the departure of de Labourdonnais from France. He won a short match against Staunton early in 1843 but in the big return match later in the year, which was virtually for the world championship, he was decisively defeated. An unsuccessful appearance at the Birmingham tournament of 1858 was his only other incursion into competitive play. Boncourt was a strong French master who drew a match with Szen in 1835.

GAME 3

BONCOURT–SAINT-AMANT

Played in Paris, 1839.

GIUOCO PIANO

1. P—K4 P—K4
2. B—B4 Kt—KB3
3. P—Q3

The normal gambit continuation of the King's Bishop's Opening is P—Q4. Now the game transposes into a quiet version of the Giuoco Piano.

3. ... B—B4
4. Kt—KB3 Kt—B3
5. P—B3 B—Kt3
6. O—O O—O
7. B—KKt5 P—Q3
8. P—QKt4

The advance of the Q side pawns in this opening was later strongly commended by Bird.

8. ... B—K3
9. QKt—Q2 P—KR3
10. B—R4 K—R2

Preparing to support a K side attack with R—KKt1.

11. P—R4 P—R3
12. K—R1 R—KKt1
13. Q—B2

While White prepares an attack in the centre with P—Q4, which would at present be answered by 13 . . ., B×B; 14 14 Kt×B, Kt×KP.

13. ... P—Kt4
14. B—KKt3 P—KR4
15. P—R3 P—R5
16. B—KR2 Kt—KR4
17. P—Q4 P—Kt5

The game has suddenly become exceedingly critical. If White replies 18 P—Q5, Black gets a very strong attack by P×Kt; 19 Kt×P, B×RP; 20 P×B, Q—B3; 21 Q—K2, Kt—K2; threatening Kt—Kt6ch.

18. B×B

Or 18 RP×P, B×B; 19 Kt×B, R×P; with variations similar to those in the actual game.

18. ... P×B
19. RP×P R×P
20. P×P P×P
21. Kt—B4 Kt—Kt6ch.

A splendid continuation, ignoring the threatened loss of the KP and continuing the attack at all costs.

22. P×Kt P×P
23. QR—Q1

Now the form of Black's attack is clear. If 23 Kt(4)×P, Kt×Kt; 24 Kt×Kt, R—R5; 25 Kt—B3, R×Bch.; 26 Kt ×R, Q—R5; while if 23 Kt (3) ×P, R—R5; 24 Kt×B, R× Bch.; 25 K—Kt1, R—R8ch.; 26 K×R, Q—R5ch. The best line was 23 Kt×B, P×Kt; 24 QR—Q1, Q—K2; 25 Q—Q2 (not R—Q3, R—R1; 26 R(B)—Q1, K—Kt3; 27 R—Q7, R×Bch.; 28 K—Kt1, R(Kt)—R5, R—Q1; 26 Q—QB2, R—R5.

23. Q—K2
24. P—Kt5

(BLACK) SAINT-AMANT

(WHITE) BONCOURT

Position before Black's 24th move.

(DIAGRAM 5)

White also plays to win; he is a piece ahead and hopes to capture another while Black goes after the condemned bishop. Nevertheless 24 Kt×B still gave him better chances.

24. R—R5
25. Kt×B

Of course not 25 P×Kt, when R×Bch., brings Black's attack to one of its successful conclusions.

25. R×Bch.
26. K—Kt1 Q—B4ch.
27. R—B2 P×Kt

Not P×Rch.; 28 K×R, P ×Kt; 29 P×Kt.

28. Kt×R

Now 28 P×Kt does not win a piece because R—R3 in reply followed by the capture on his KB2 leaves him the exchange down. He must therefore take the rook while it is still there.

28. P×P
29. P×P R—KB1
30. Kt—B3

And now not 30 P×Kt, R× R; with a winning game, Black brings all his pieces on to good squares before recovering the piece.

30. Kt—R4
31. Q—K2 Kt—B5
32. Kt—Kt5ch. K—Kt3
33. Kt—B3

If 33 Kt×P, Q×Rch.; 34 Q×Q, P×Qch.; 35 K—B1, Kt—K6ch.; winning.

33. R—B5
34. R—Q3 P×Rch.
35. Q×P Q×Qch.
36. K×Q R×P
37. R—Q7 R—B5
38. R×P

That this move, which looks perfectly good, actually loses shows how carefully Black has calculated the whole of the preceding play. On the other hand after the better 38 K—Kt3, R—B2; White can hardly save the ending, for if 39 R—Q1, P—K5; 40 Kt—Q4, P—K4; 41 Kt—K6, K—B4; 42 Kt—Q8, R—Kt2ch.; 43 K—B2, P—K6ch.; 44 K—Kt1, P—K7; 43 R—K1, R—Q2; or 39 R×R, K×R; 40 K—Kt4, K—B3; threatening Kt—Q3.

38. P—K5
39. K—Kt3 P×Kt

A brilliant conclusion to a tremendous game.

40. P×P P—K4
Resigns.

H. Staunton (1810–1874) was the only British player to become world champion, a position he was generally considered to have attained after his victory over Saint-Amant in Paris in 1843. His record in match play is unequalled by any other British player, among his other conquests being Popert, Cochrane, Horwitz, Harrwitz and Jaenisch. He was a profound theorist, author of a number of books, the editor of the first successful chess magazine and a great pioneer, organising the first game by telegraph and the first international tournament. A weak heart limited his capacity for strenuous play after 1849.

GAME 4

STAUNTON–SAINT-AMANT

2nd match game, London, 1843.

KING'S BISHOP'S OPENING

1. P—K4 P—K4
2. B—B4 Kt—KB3
3. P—Q4 Q—K2

Better was P×P at once.

4. Kt—QB3 P×P
5. Q×P Kt—B3
6. Q—K3 Kt—K4
7. B—Kt3 P—B3
8. P—KR3 P—Q3
9 KKt—K2 P—KR3
10. P—B4 Kt—Kt3
11. O—O B—K3
12. P—B5 B×B
13. RP×B Kt—K4
14. R×P

As a result of Black's indifferent opening White has now much the better game.

14. R—QKt1
15. B—Q2 Kt(4)—Q2
16. KR—R1 Q—Q1
17. Kt—R4 B—K2
18. Kt—Q4

Not 18 B—R5, P—QKt3.

18. O—O
19. B—R5 Q—B1
20. Kt—Kt6

But now White rushes matters too fast, and Black is able to counter the flank attack with a thrust in the centre which recovers the pawn. 20 Kt—KB3 first was better.

20. Kt×Kt
21. B×Kt P—B4
22. Kt—B3 Q—B3
23. B—R5 Kt×P
24. P—QKt4

Losing a pawn, but if 24 R—K1, P—Q4; 25 P—B4, B—Kt4; 26 Kt×B, Kt×Kt; and Black controls the K file.

24. P—Q4
25. P—B3 KR—K1
26. P—Kt5

Forced by the threat of P—QKt3. Black could safely continue Q×P; 27 B—B7, QR—B1; 28 P—B4, Q×BP; 29 R×P, Kt—B3. The line chosen is less decisive but good enough. It is now Black who calls the tune.

26. Q—Q3
27. P—B4 B—B3
28. Q—Q3 P—QKt3
29. B—K1 P—Q5
30. Kt—Q2 Kt×Kt
31. B×Kt B—Q1
32. R—KB1 B—Kt4

If B—B2; 33 B—B4, showing that he should have played B—Kt4 a move earlier.

33. B×B P×B
34. P—B6 P—Kt3

If P×P; 35 Q—B5. Now Black threatens R—K6.

35. Q—KB3 P—Q6
36. Q—Kt4 Q—K4

(BLACK) SAINT-AMANT

(WHITE) STAUNTON

Position before White's 37th move.

(Diagram 6)

37. R×P

Just as Black appears to be consolidating his advantage, White returns to the attack with a splendid fighting combination which all but secures the draw. Black cannot reply 37 . . ., K×R; 38 Q—Q7ch.,

R—K2; 39 P×R dis.ch., K—Kt1; 40 Q—Q8ch., K—R2; 41 R—B7ch., K—R3; 42 Q—B8ch., winning.

37. Q—K6ch.
38. K—R1 Q—K7
39. R—Kt7ch. K—B1
40. R—B7ch. K×R
41. Q—Q7ch. R—K2
42. Q×Rch.

Of course if now 42 P×Rdis. ch., Q×Rch.

42. Q×Q
43. P×Qdis.ch. K×P
44. K—Kt1

If 44 R—Q1, R—Q1; 45 R—Q2, R—Q5; 46 P—QKt3, K—K3; 47 K—Kt1, K—K4; 48 K—B2, K—K5; 49 K—K1, K—K6; with advantage.

44. R—Q1
45. R—Q1 R—Q5
46. P—QKt3 P—Q7
47. K—B2 R—Q6
48. K—K2 R×KtP
49. R×P R—QB6
50. R—Q5 R×BP
51. R×KtP K—B3

K—B2, to hold the QKtP, is correct, as he discovers.

52. R—Q5 K—K3
53. R—Kt5 K—B2
54. R—Q5 R—QKt5
55. R—Q7ch. K—K3
56. R—QB7 K—B4
57. R—B7ch. K—Kt4
58. K—Q3 R×P
59. K—B4 R—Kt5ch.
60. K—Q5 R—Kt7
61. P—Kt4 R—Kt5
62. R—B7 R—Kt6
63. R—KR7 R—Kt5
64. R—QB7 P—B5
65. K—Q4 P—Kt4
66. R—B5ch. K—R5
67. R—B6 K—Kt4
68. R—B5ch.

(BLACK) SAINT-AMANT

(WHITE) STAUNTON

Position before Black's 68th move.

(DIAGRAM 7)

68. K—R3

Up to this point Black has played with exemplary precision and has foiled all White's efforts to ensure the draw, but now he errs in allowing White to obtain a passed pawn. The winning line was 68 . . ., K—R5; 69 R—B6, P—B6 dis.ch.; 70 K×P, R—B5ch.; 71 R×R, P×R; 72 K×P, K×P; 73 P—Kt5, K—Kt5.

69. P—R4 R—Kt6
70. P—R5 R—Kt6
71. P×P

Better than 71 R×KtP, R×Pch.; 72 K—B3, P×P.

71. R×Pch.
72. K—B3 R—Kt6ch.
73. K—Q4 R—Q6ch.
74. K—K4 R—QKt6
75. K—B5

Now the draw is certain.

75. R—Kt8
76. K—B6 R—B8ch.
77. K—K6 R—QKt8
78. K—B7 R—B8ch.
79. K—K6 R—K8ch.
80. K—B7 R—B8ch.
81. K—K6 K×P
82. R×KtP P—B6
83. R—QB5 R—QB8
84. K—Q5 P—B7
85. K—B6

The way White now shuffles down the file without allowing Black a check is amusing. So magnificent a struggle in an off-hand match made a later set match a virtual certainty.

85. K—B3
86. R—B4 K—K4
87. K—B5 K—B4
88. R—B3 K—K5
89. K—B4 K—B5
90. K—Kt3 Drawn.

B. Horwitz was one of the most eminent of the famous and brilliant school of seven German masters, known as the Pleiades, which flourished between 1836 and 1846. He resided in England after 1845 and it was during this latter part of his career that he was associated with Kling in the compilation of their famous book of end-game studies.

H. E. Bird (1830–1908), a genial and popular British master, played regularly in international tournaments between 1851 and 1899. A player of dashing originality, his success was limited by a predilection for risky and unusual openings, his best results being 1st at London, 1879 and 1889, equal 2nd at Hereford, 1885, and 3rd at Philadelphia, 1877. He met both Morphy and Anderssen, and contested matches with Steinitz and Lasker; against Steinitz in 1866, just after that player had become world champion, he only lost by the odd game in 17.

GAME 5

BIRD–HORWITZ

2nd game, 1st round, London tournament, 1851.

RUY LOPEZ

1. P—K4 P—K4
2. Kt—KB3 Kt—QB3
3. B—Kt5 Kt—B3
4. P—Q4 Kt×QP

Allowing White too much scope. P×P was better.

5. Kt×Kt P×Kt
6. P—K5 Kt—Q4
7. O—O

An unnecessary gambit. Q×P was strong and took full advantage of Black's 4th move.

7. B—B4
8. P—QB3 P—QR3
9. B—QB4

B—K2, playing to win the centre pawn, is answered by Q—R5.

9. Kt—Kt3
10. B—Kt3 P×P
11. Kt×P O—O
12. Kt—K4

Now and in the following moves White plays for attack at all costs; the more solid R—K1 does not achieve all it might because of his failure to take the pawn on the 7th move. Black defends skilfully after his initial weak play.

12. Q—K2
13. Q—R5 P—Q3
14. B—Kt5 Q×P
15. QR—K1 Kt—Q4

By sacrificing another pawn White has developed a dangerous attack and threatens Kt—B6ch., winning the queen. Black finds a brilliant defence.

16. Kt×B

Now Kt—B6ch., would lose a piece.

16. Kt—B3
17. Q—R4

If 17 R×Q, Kt×Q; 18 R moves, P×Kt; recovering the piece with a winning game.

17. Q×Kt
18. B×Kt P×B
19. R—K3 B—B4
20. Q×P B—Kt3
21. R—Kt3 Q—K4
22. Q—R4 Q×P

Satisfied that he can hold the threat to his bishop, for which he has an ingenious defence prepared. The likely looking KR—K1 only gives a draw after 23 P—B4, Q—K2; 24 Q—R6, Q—B1; 25 Q—Kt5, Q—K2 (not P—KR3; 26 Q×Bch.).

23. P—B4 Q—Q5ch.

Pinning the BP on the queen.

24. K—R1 QR—K1
25. Q—Kt5 Q—B7

Beautifully conceived. The rook is to be forced off the KKt file, so that the queen will be left undefended and a further pin made possible on the diagonal. White cannot reply R—KKt1 because of R—K8.

26. R—KB3 Q—Q7
27. P—KR4 P—B3

A waiting move, but K—Kt2 was better. He has another pretty defence against the advance of the RP, which also hinges upon the pin of the KBP, but he cannot put it into operation until P—R5 leaves the queen undefended again.

28. P—R5 R—K4

(BLACK) HORWITZ

(WHITE) BIRD

Position before White's 29th move.

(DIAGRAM 8)

Apparently turning the tables entirely for if the queen moves, R×Pch. But though both pawn advances are held White finds another gallant, if not quite sound, method of keeping his flag flying.

29. B×Pch. R×B

Forced. If K—Kt2; 30 P—R6ch., K×B (K—R1; 31 Q—B6 Mate); 31 P×R dis.ch., and 32 Q×Q.

30. Q—Q8ch. R—B1

Not K—Kt2; 31 P×R, winning the exchange.

31. Q×Rch. K×Q
32. P×Rdis.ch. K—Kt2

An error. After K—K2; 33 P×B, RP×P; 34 P×Pch., Q×P; Black's extra pawns should win.

33. P×B QP×P

A graver error, and strange coming from a famous end-game composer. Now the king will be entirely exposed. Black should not hope after his previous move for more than a perpetual check; in playing to win he loses. Correct was K×P; 34 P×P (not R—B6ch., which is answered by K—Kt2; 35 R—B7ch., K—Kt1; and not by K—Kt4; 35 R(1)—B5ch., K—Kt5; 36 R—B4ch., Q×R; 37 R×Qch., K×R; 38 P×P, wins).

34. P×P K×P
35. K—R2 P—K5
36. R—R3ch. K—Kt3
37. R—Kt3ch. K—R2

If K—R4; 38 R—B8, threatening R—R8 Mate.

38. R—B7ch. K—R3
39. R—B6ch. K—R4

If K—R2; 40 R(6)—Kt6, threatening R(6)—Kt4.

40. R—B8 Q—Q5
41. R—R8ch.

Prettily destroying Black's position. But White's task even now presents difficulties.

41. Q×R
42. R—R3ch. K—Kt5
43. R×Q K—B5
44. R—B8ch. K—K6
45. K—Kt3

K—Kt1 was much stronger. Now Black comes almost within reach of victory again.

45. P—B4
46. R—QKt8 P—Kt4
47. R—Kt6 P—B5
48. R×RP P—B6
49. R—QB6 K—Q7
50. K—B4 P—K6
51. R—Q6ch. K—K7

If White had played 45 K—Kt1, and 50 K—B1, Black would have been forced into 51 . . ., K—B7; when 52 K—K2, wins.

52. P—Kt4 K—B7
53. R—KR6 P—K7
54. R—R2ch. K—B8
55. K—B3

The saving clause and a pretty one. If now P—K8=Q or P—B7; 56 R—R1 Mate.

55. P—K8=Ktch.
56. K—K3 Kt—Kt7ch.

If P—B7; 57 R—R1ch., K—Kt2; 58 R×Kt. A cut and thrust game of exceptional brilliance all through.

57. R×Kt K×R
58. P—Kt5 P—Kt5
59. K—Q3 Resigns.

von Heydebrandt und der Lasa (1819–1899), the most brilliant and the strongest of the German "Pleiades," was prevented after 1840 from participating in competition play by his duties as an Ambassador of the Prussian court. He always retained an interest in the game, but an unfinished series against Staunton in 1853 was his only play of a competitive nature.

GAME 6

VON DER LASA–STAUNTON

2nd match game,
Brussels, 1853.

KING'S BISHOP'S OPENING

1. P—K4 P—K4
2. P—Q4 P×P
3. B—QB4 Kt—KB3
4. P—K5

Modern practice is Kt—KB3. White's method of play is answered by Staunton with crushing logic.

4. P—Q4
5. B—Kt3 Kt—K5
6. Kt—K2 P—QB4
7. O—O Kt—QB3
8. P—KB3 Kt—Kt4
9. Kt—B4 P—B5
10. B—R4 B—QB4
11. K—R1 Kt—K3
12. P—QKt4 B—Kt3

If B×P; 13 Kt×Kt, B×Kt; 14 Q×P.

13. Kt×Kt B×Kt
14. P—B4 B—KB4
15. B—R3 O—O
16. Kt—Q2 P—Q6
17. P—Kt5 Kt—K2

Safe enough, but better was von der Lasa's suggestion 17 . . ., P×P; 18 B×P, B×B; 19 Q×B, Kt—Q5; 20 Q—Q1, R—K1. Staunton even recommended the sacrificial line 17 . . ., Kt—Q5; 18 B×R, Kt—K7 (threatening Q—R5 and Kt—Kt6); 19 Q—K1, Q×B; 20 P×P, P×P; 21 B—Q1, B—Q5; 22 R—QKt1, Q—R6.

18. P×P B×P
19. R—B3 R—K1
20. B—B2 B×B

If B—Kt3; 21 P—Kt4.

21. Q×B Kt—Kt3
22. R—Q1 Q—B1

Kt×P was threatened.

23. B—Kt2 Q—QB4
24. Kt—Kt1 QR—Q1
25. Kt—R3 Q—K2
26. R—R3 P—KR3
27. R—KB1 Q—B4
28. P—K6

In a difficult position White produces a magnificent move to make a fight of it. Clearly the pawn cannot be captured without loss of a piece, and Black's Kt×P would now be answered by 29 P×Pch., K×P; 30 R×Ktch. Moreover, White in turn

(BLACK) STAUNTON

(WHITE) VON DER LASA

Position before Black's 28th move.

(DIAGRAM 9)

now threatens 29 P×Pch., K×P; 30 Q—B5ch.

28. R—Q3
29. Q—B3 P—B3
30. R—Kt3

If 30 P—B5, Kt—B5; 31 R—Kt3, Kt—Q6; 32 R×Pch., K—R1; and now if 33 Q×KBP, Q—Kt8ch.

30. R(3)×P

The saving clause and a splendid one. 31 P—B5 would now be answered by R—K6, and 31 R×Kt by the beautiful move Q—B7.

31. Kt—B2 Kt×P
32. Q—B3 Q—B2
33. R—Kt4

Q×Kt would allow mate. His brave effort is now over and Staunton winds up powerfully.

33.		P—Kt4
34.	P—Kt3	P—KR4
35.	R×Kt	P×R
36.	Q×RP	Q—R2
37.	Q—Kt4ch.	K—B2
38.	Q×P	Q×Kt
39.	B×P	Q—K5ch.

Resigns.

A. Anderssen (1818–1879) did not become prominent until he was 30 years of age, but then rapidly became known as the most brilliant combinative player of his time, and was regarded as the world champion from his victory at the London tournament of 1851 until his loss of a match to Steinitz in 1866 ; the only break in this period of supremacy was when Morphy was playing. Among his other great tournament victories were London, 1862, and Baden-Baden, 1870.

P. Morphy (1837–1884), the greatest master of the open game, has claims to be regarded as the greatest player of all time. His career was limited almost entirely to the years 1857 to 1859, in which time he defeated every player he met including Anderssen, Lowenthal and Harrwitz. In style he was sound and deep but capable of exceptional brilliance when opportunity offered. After a meteoric career he retired completely, being afflicted with a form of melancholia.

GAME 7

ANDERSSEN–MORPHY

2nd match game,
Paris, 1858.

Ruy Lopez

1.	P—K4	P—K4
2.	Kt—KB3	Kt—QB3
3.	B—Kt5	P—QR3

Introducing for the first time the defence now named after him.

4.	B—R4	Kt—B3
5.	P—Q3	

Lines involving P—B3 and P—Q4 were only developed later.

5.		B—B4
6.	P—B3	P—QKt4
7.	B—B2	

Better was B—Kt3 to hinder Black's P—Q4.

7.		P—Q4
8.	P×P	Kt×P
9.	P—KR3	O—O

10. O—O P—R3
11. P—Q4

Anderssen prepares to attack along the diagonal. The diagonal could be opened without allowing an isolated pawn by 11 Kt×P, Kt×Kt; 12 P—Q4, but the pawn is a bait in Anderssen's plan.

11. P×P
12. P×P B—Kt3
13. Kt—B3 Kt(Q)—Kt5
14. B—Kt1 B—K3

Refusing to be tempted. If 14..., Kt×QP (B×P; 15 Kt—K2, B—Kt3; 16 P—R3, Kt—Q4; 17 Q—B2, wins); 15 Kt×Kt, B×Kt (Q×Kt; 16 Q—B3, B—K3; 17 P—R3, Kt—Q4; 18 R—Q1); 16 Q—B3, B—K3; 17 Q—K4, and White has a very dangerous attack. Zukertort has shown that Black can probably just weather it, but over the board it would be a dangerous venture.

15. P—R3 Kt—Q4
16. Kt—K2

Threatening Q—B2. The alternative 16 Kt×P would be answered by Kt—B3; 17 Kt—B3, Kt×P.

16. Kt—B3
17. B—K3 R—K1
18. Kt—Kt3 B—B5
[Diagram 10]

19. Kt—B5

Morphy has now manœuvred himself into a position where the isolated pawn can be captured

(BLACK) MORPHY

(WHITE) ANDERSSEN

Position before White's 19th move.

(DIAGRAM 10)

with impunity, for if 19 R—K1, Kt×P; 20 Kt×Kt, B×Kt; 21 B×B, R×Rch.; 22 Q×R., Q×B. White therefore takes his courage in both hands and sacrifices the exchange. The only alternative was B—Q3.

19. B×R
20. Q×B Kt—K2
21. Kt(3)—R4 Kt×Kt
22. Kt×Kt Q—Q2
23. B×P

The counter-attack begins to gather weight. A simple and good reply was 23 . . ., B×P.

23. P×B
24. Q—B1 B×P

What was good a move earlier is now inferior, and on such small nuances do success and failure so often depend. The correct line, given by Zukertort was 24 . . ., Kt—R2; 25 Q×

RP, P—KB3; 26 B—R2ch., (Kt—R4, R—K8ch.; 27 K—R2, R×B), K—R1; 27 Kt—R4, R—KKt1; 28 B×R, K×B. Even so Morphy's line is not obviously inferior by any means.

25. Q×RP R—K8ch.
26. K—R2 Kt—K5
27. B×Kt

And it is only this brilliant continuation which shows up the weakness of Black's 24th move. Now if 27 . . ., R×R; White can force a draw by 28 Kt—K7ch., Q×Kt; 29 B—R7ch., or he can play an ending with two minor pieces against a rook after 28 Kt×B, Q—Q3ch.; 29 Q×Q, P×Q; 30 B×R. Once again the simple text move seems to leave White no future.

27. R×B
28. Q—Kt5ch. K—B1
29. Q—R6ch. K—K1
30. Kt×B

And once again White finds a surprise move to keep his game alive. If now 30 . . ., Q×Kt (R×Kt; 31 R—K1ch., wins); 31 Q—B6ch., K—K2; 32 Q×QR, with a probable draw.

30. Q—Q3ch.
31. Q×Q P×Q
32. R—Q1 K—B1

Black has fought his way through all White's brilliancies into an ending where he is the exchange ahead, only to find that White can nevertheless hold everything.

33. R—Q2 R(R)—K1
34. P—KKt4 R(1)—K4
35. P—B3 R—K8
36. P—KR4 R—Q4
37. K—Kt3 P—R4
38. P—R5 K—Kt1
39. K—B2 R—K1
40. K—Kt3 K—R2
41. K—B4 R—K2
42. K—Kt3 P—B3
43. K—B4 R—K1
44. K—Kt3 R—K2

Drawn.

Black has no target for his rooks and he cannot play K—R3 because of Kt—B5ch. Equally White can do nothing with his K side pawns so long as Black sits tight.

W. Steinitz (1836–1900), a Bohemian Jew, was world champion from 1866 to 1894, and the first great master of position play. He was an outstanding match player, and besides winning against Anderssen he won among others three matches against Blackburne, two against Zukertort, two against Tchigorin, one against Mackenzie and one against Gunsberg; he was finally beaten by Lasker. His tournament record, though slightly less impressive, included 1st prizes at London, 1871, Vienna, 1873, and New York, 1894, an equal 1st at Vienna, 1882, and 2nd prizes at Dundee, 1867, Baden-Baden, 1870, London, 1883, and St. Petersburg, 1896.

GAME 8

ANDERSSEN–STEINITZ

3rd match game,
London, 1866.

EVANS GAMBIT

1. P—K4 P—K4
2. Kt—KB3 Kt—QB3
3. B—B4 B—B4
4. P—QKt4 B×P
5. P—B3 B—B4
6. P—Q4 P×P
7. O—O P—Q6

The Compromised Defence by 7 . . ., P×P, though possibly playable, leads to too difficult a game for over-the-board play. The text move has the advantage that White is denied the square QB3 for his knight, a form of development which seems essential if White is to get up a good attack.

8. Q×P

But this makes even less of the position than usual. Either Q—Kt3 or Kt—Kt5 was preferable, hindering Black's castling.

8. P—Q3
9. B—KKt5 KKt—K2
10. QKt—Q2 P—KR3
11. B—R4 O—O
12. Kt—Kt3 B—Kt3
13. P—KR3 B—K3
14. QR—Q1

Preventing P—Q4.

14. Q—Q2
15. B—Q5 Kt—Kt3
16. B—Kt3 QR—K1
17. P—B4 B×B
18. KP×B QKt—K4
19. Kt×Kt Kt×Kt
20. Q—QB3 Kt—Kt3

[Diagram 11]

21. P—B5

White has slightly the better development for his pawn and now starts an ingenious attack which turns a material disadvantage to a material advantage.

(BLACK) STEINITZ

(WHITE) ANDERSSEN

Position before White's 21st move.

(DIAGRAM 11)

21. P×P
22. Kt×P Q—B4

If 22 . . ., B×Kt ; 23 Q×B, R—B1 (R—K2 ; 24 P—Q6, P×P ; 25 B×P) ; 24 Q×RP.

23. Kt×P R—K7

Both players go all out for attack ; Black allows White to win a pawn on the Q side rather than indulge in difficult and elaborate defensive measures.

24. P—Q6 P×P
25. Kt×P Q—K3
26. P—QR4 B—Q1

If 26 . . ., P—QR4 ; 27 Kt—Kt5, threatening 28 R—Q6.

27. Q—B5 P—B4
28. Q×RP P—B5
29. B—R2 Kt—R5
30. Q—Kt7 Q—Kt3
31. R—Q4

The position is extremely critical now owing to Black's mating threat. The text proves to be merely loss of time which puts his knight in chancery, though the alternative 31 Q—Q5ch., is not entirely satisfactory after 31 . . ., K—R1 (K—R2 ; 32 Q—Q3) ; 32 Kt—B7ch., K—R2 ; 33 Q—Q3 (Kt×B, R×Kt), R—K5 ; 34 P—Kt4, B—K2 (P×P e.p. ; 35 B×P, or R×Kt ; 35 Q×B) ; 35 Kt—Q6, B×Kt ; 36 Q×B. Kt—B6ch. ; 37 K—R1, R—B3 ; 38 Q—Q7, Kt—K4 ; 39 Q—Kt5, P—KR4 ; for White's extra pawn is of less value than Black's attacking chances.

31. B—Kt3
32. R(4)—Q1

R—Kt4 would allow B×Pch. ; 33 R×B, R×R ; 34 K×R, Q—B7ch. ; 35 K—B1, Q—Q6ch. (not P—B6 ; 36 R—Kt2) ; 36 K—Kt1, Q×Kt ; with advantage.

32. R—K3

Now White's troubles are severe, for if 33 Kt—Kt5, R—QB3 ; 34 P—KKt3, P×P ; 35 B×P, Q×Bch. White therefore offers the QRP to draw the Black bishop off the dangerous diagonal.

33. P—R5 B—B4
[Diagram 12]

34. P—R6

Black is not to be drawn, but now White has a chance of utilising his pawn which he seizes in splendid style. If in reply

(BLACK) STEINITZ

(WHITE) ANDERSSEN

Position before White's 34th move.

(DIAGRAM 12)

34 . . ., B×Kt ; 35 P—R7, R—K2 ; 36 P—R8=Q, winning.

34. R—K2

The thrusts and counter-thrusts are most exciting. Black delays the capture of the knight until he has attended to the threat of P—R7, White being always hampered by the necessity of keeping his queen on the long diagonal.

35. Q—Q5ch. K—R1
36. P—R7

White still cannot rescue his knight because of the answer 36 . . ., R—Q2 ; forcing the queen off the diagonal. He therefore sacrifices the QRP in order to break out of Black's grip.

36. B×P

If R×P ; 37 KR—K1, B×Kt ; 38 R—K6, Q×Pch. ; 39 Q×Q, Kt×Q ; 40 R(6)×B, Kt—R5 ; 41 R—Q8, and the threat to Black's BP enables White to draw.

37. KR—K1 R×Rch.
38. R×R K—R2

A move as subtle as White's defence has been fine. He sees that the forced exchange of queens is imminent and evolves a plan to continue the attack without the queen ; the immediate threat of R—Q1 is only subsidiary to his real plan.

39. Q—K4 R—B3
40. Kt—Kt5 R—K3

The point, temporarily giving up the bishop. The play on both sides is most brilliant.

41. Q×Qch. R×Q
42. Kt×B R×Pch.
43. K—R1 R×Bch.
44. K×R Kt—B6ch.
45. K—Kt2 Kt×Rch.
46. K—B1 Kt—Q6
47. Kt—B6

Now follows a difficult knight end-game in which it is doubtful whether Black's extra pawn is sufficient to win.

47. K—Kt3
48. K—K2 Kt—B4
49. K—B3 Kt—K3
50. Kt—K5ch. K—B4
51. Kt—Q3

A serious error, as P. W. Sergeant has shown, for the knight is soon reduced to abject helplessness, whereas after Kt—B4 it would retain its freedom of action. From this moment White's chances of saving the game vanish.

51.		P—Kt3
52.	Kt—K1	Kt—Q5ch.
53.	K—Kt2	K—K5
54.	K—B1	P—B6
55.	K—Kt1	P—Kt4
56.	K—R2	P—R4
57.	K—Kt3	Kt—B4ch.
58.	K—R2	P—Kt5
59.	P×P	P×P
60.	K—Kt1	

Even now the White knight cannot come back into play, for if 60 Kt—B2, K—Q6; 61 Kt—Kt4ch., K—K7; 62 K—Kt1, P—Kt6; winning.

60.		K—Q5
61.	Kt—B2ch.	K—Q6
62.	Kt—R3	

Atkins has shown that no better was 62 Kt—Kt4ch., because of K—K7; 63 Kt—Q5, P—Kt6; 64 Kt—B4ch., K—K8; 65 Kt—Kt2ch., P×Kt; 66 P×P, Kt—K6; 67 P—Kt4, K—K7; 68 P—Kt5, K—B6; 69 P—Kt6, Kt—B4; winning.

62.		P—Kt6
63.	Kt—Kt5	

Of course not 63 P×P, K—K7.

63.		P—Kt7

and wins.

For after 64 K—R2 (Kt—R3, Kt—Kt6), K—K7; 65 K—Kt1, K—K8; 66 Kt—R3 (Kt—B3, Kt—Kt6 preventing Kt—K4), Kt—K6 (preventing Kt—B2ch.); 67 Kt—Kt1 (Kt—Kt5, Kt—Kt5; 68 Kt—B3, Kt×P), Kt—Kt5; 68 Kt—R3, Kt×P; 69 Kt—B2ch., K—Q7; winning.

J. H. Zukertort (1842–1888) was a Pole who lived in England from 1871. He was a very gifted and very brilliant player but of a nervous temperament and indifferent stamina. He scored quite remarkable wins in tournament play, including 1st prizes at the great tournament at Paris, 1878, and London, 1883, 2nd prize at Berlin, 1881, and equal 2nd at Leipzig, 1877. He was for a long time regarded as Steinitz's only great rival but in their two matches, in 1872 and 1886, his stamina proved insufficient, though he never understood why he failed to win.

GAME 9

ZUKERTORT–STEINITZ

1st match game, London, 1872.

GIUOCO PIANO

1.	P—K4	P—K4
2.	Kt—KB3	Kt—QB3
3.	B—B4	B—B4

4. P—B3 Kt—B3
5. P—Q4 P×P
6. P×P B—Kt3

Less aggressive than the usual B—Kt5ch. as White can now play 7 Kt—B3 and Black must give up all hope of playing the QP forward two squares. It should be remembered that the Moller Attack, preventing Black's P—Q4 even after 6 . . ., B—Kt5ch.; had not yet been invented.

7. O—O

Preferring to precipitate an immediate crisis in the centre rather than follow orthodox lines.

7. Kt×KP
8. R—K1 O—O

Less favourable would be P—Q4; 9 B×P, Q×B; 10 Kt—B3, as the Black king is then still in the centre.

9. R×Kt P—Q4
10. B×P Q×B
11. Kt—B3 Q—Q1
12. P—Q5 Kt—K2
13. B—Kt5 P—KB3
14. Q—Kt3

The force of White's attack begins to be revealed. If 14 . . ., P×B; 15 P—Q6 dis.ch., R—B2; 16 P×Kt, Q—K1; 17 Kt×P, B—KB4; 18 R—K5, with advantage. The simplest reply is 14 . . ., K—R1; avoiding all complications on the dangerous diagonal, but Black allows White's attack to continue in the belief that the pressure cannot be maintained.

14. R—B2
15. QR—K1 K—B1

(BLACK) STEINITZ

(WHITE) ZUKERTORT

Position before White's 16th move.

(DIAGRAM 13)

16. P—Q6

Continuing the attack with unabated energy. If 16 . . ., Q×P; 17 R—Q1, threatening R—Q8 Mate.

16. P×P
17. Kt—Q5 Kt×Kt

If now 17 . . ., P×B; 18 R×Kt, R×R (against R—K8ch.); 19 Kt×R, B—Q2; 20 Kt×P, with advantage.

18. Q×Kt

Now not 18 R—K8ch., Q×R; 19 R×Qch., K×R; 20 Q×Kt, P×B; and Black has two rooks and a minor piece for the queen.

Moreover, White cannot continue 21 Kt×P because of R×P. After the text move White threatens 19 Q×Pch., and if Q×Q ; 20 R—K8 Mate.

18. B—Q2

Black has nothing better than to sacrifice the QP, for 18 . . ., B—QB4 is answered by 19 Kt—K5, and 18 . . ., B—B2 by 19 R—K8ch., Q×R ; 20 R×Qch., K×R ; 21 B—B4, with severe pressure on Black's position.

19. Q×Pch. K—Kt1
20. Kt—K5 B×Pch.

A counter-attack just in time and a very pretty one. If in reply 21 K×B, P×Kt dis.ch. ; 22 K—Kt1, Q×B ; winning.

21. K—R1 B×R
22. Kt×R K×Kt
23. Q—Q5ch. K—Kt3

The key move of Black's defence. 23 . . ., K—B1 would fail against 24 B—B4, threatening B—Q6 Mate.

24. R×B B—B3

But here Black misses the best line. P×B could at last be played for if 25 R—Q1, R—B1 ; 26 Q×B, Q×Q ; 27 R×Q, R—B8ch.

25. Q×Q R×Q
26. B—K3

The bishop has been *en prise* for 12 moves, but the time has come to withdraw it at last. Black has emerged from his hammering a pawn ahead but the bishops of opposite colours indicate a probable draw.

26. K—B2
27. K—Kt1 P—KKt4
28. R—K2 P—QR3
29. R—Q2 R—K1

An exchange of rooks would be a surrender of his last thin chance of winning, and sure enough White makes an error on his very next move, allowing Black to win another pawn or force the bishops off.

30. K—B2 B×P
31. B×P P×B
32. K×B K—B3
33. K—B3 P—KR4
34. P—KR4

In a technically lost position White is not prepared to allow Black to proceed along known lines. Instead he throws every possible complication in Black's way. If 34 . . ., P—Kt5ch. ; 35 K—B4, and Black's progress is barred, for if 35 . . ., R—KKt1 ; 36 R—Kt2, or if 35 . . ., K—Kt 3 ; 36 R—Q5, or if 35 . . ., K—K3 ; 36 K—Kt5.

34. P×P
35. R—Q4 K—Kt4
36. R—Q5ch. K—Kt3
37. R—Q6ch. K—B4
38. R—Q4

Now if R—Q5ch., R—K4. Black's king has therefore advanced one rank as a result of the manœuvre of the last three moves.

38. P—R6
39. R—KR4 K—Kt4

40. R×P P—R5
41. K—B2

The only move to get the rook back into play, for if 41 R—R2 then R—B1ch.; 42 K—Kt2, K—Kt5.

41. R—B1
42. R—Kt3 R—B7ch
43. K—Kt1 P—Kt4
44. P—R4

The second rook's pawn to be sacrificed.

44. P×P
45. R—Kt4 R—B8ch.
46. K—R2 R—QKt8
47. R×QRP R×Pch.
48. K—R3 R—Kt6ch.
49. K—R2 R—Kt3
50. K—R3 K—B4

Successfully and elegantly forcing the issue at last. R—R3 was a much slower process.

51. K×P R—Kt3
52. K—R5 R—K3
53. R—R5ch. K—K5
54. K—Kt5

A blunder, but the result is inevitable after 54 K—Kt4, R—Kt3ch.; 55 K—R5, R—QB3; 56 K—Kt4, K—Q5; 57 K—B4, K—B5; 58 K—K4, K—Kt5; 59 R—R1, P—R4.

54. R—K4ch.
Resigns.

J. Mason (1849–1905), born in Ireland but taken to America in infancy, sprang into prominence when he won the American championship in 1877. His style was simple and elegant and on his day he was the equal of the strongest players. His play was, however, uneven, his best results being 2nd at London, 1892, equal 2nd at Hamburg, 1885, 3rd at Vienna, 1882, and equal 3rd at Bradford, 1888. He won matches against Bird, Mackenzie and Blackburne. He was an extremely popular chess author.

GAME 10

MASON–ZUKERTORT

London tournament, 1883.

QUEEN'S GAMBIT DECLINED

1. P—QB4 P—K3
2. P—K3 Kt—KB3
3. Kt—KB3 P—Q4
4. P—Q4 B—K2
5. Kt—B3 O—O
6. B—Q3 P—QKt3
7. P×P P×P
8. Kt—K5 B—Kt2
9. O—O P—B4
10. B—Q2

A better development is by P—QKt3 and B—Kt2.

10. Kt—B3
11. Kt×Kt

Better would be P—B4. The text merely helps Black to mobilise his Q side by enabling him to dispense with the usual P—QR3 on his 13th move.

11. B×Kt
12. R—B1

B—Kt5 will not delay Black, for then B—Kt2; 13 R—B1, P—QR3; 14 B—Q3, P—B5; leading in one move more to the position reached in the actual game.

12. P—B5
13. B—Kt1 P—QKt4
14. Kt—K2 P—Kt5
15. Kt—Kt3 P—QR4
16. R—K1

The natural reaction to Black's Q side push is to play P—K4 as soon as possible, but the text surprisingly loses the exchange by preventing the QR from going to K1 later. Much better was Q—K2.

16. P—R5
17. Kt—B5

Loss of material being inevitable, he plays for a K side attack.

17. P—R6
18. P—K4

Not 18 P×P, P—B6; and wins.

18. RP×P
19. R—B2 B—R5

White's 16th move comes home to roost at last.

20. P—K5 Kt—K1

20 . . ., B×R; 21 B×B, would merely be a transposition of moves. The text is the only knight move to win the exchange, although other moves still give Black an advantage, as for instance Kt—K5; 21 Q—Kt4, P—Kt3; 22 B—R6, B×R; 23 B×R, KB×B; 24 B×B, R×P.

21. Q—Kt4 B×R
22. B×B R—R3

Deciding after all that discretion is the better part of valour. He plays to return the exchange in order to break up White's dangerous attack.

23. Kt—R6ch. R×Kt

He would be better off playing to hold his material advantage by K—R1; 24 Q—B5, P—Kt3; 25 Kt×Pch., K—Kt 1.; 26 Kt×Q, P×Q; 27 Kt—Kt7, R×P; 28 B—R6, Kt—Kt2.

24. B×R Q—R4
25. R—KB1

White is forced back. He cannot play B—Q2 because of P—Kt6; 26 B×Q, P×B; winning.

25. Q×P
26. Q—B5 P—Kt3

[Diagram 14]

27. Q—Q7

In this apparently desperate predicament White still finds

(BLACK) ZUKERTORT

(WHITE) MASON

Position before White's 27th move.

(DIAGRAM 14)

means of attack. Black cannot save his bishop, for if B—R5; 28 P—Kt3, P—Kt6; 29 B—Kt1. In addition the rook is attacked.

27.		P—Kt6
28.	Q×B	Kt—Kt2
29.	B—Kt1	P—B6

Pretty play. White cannot answer 30 B×Q because of P×B; 31 Q—Kt4, P—R8=Q; 32 Q×BP, Q×Rch. Now Black recovers his bishop at least.

30.	Q—B5	P—B7
31.	B×P	Kt—K3

He finds after all that P×B probably only draws after 32 Q×BP, R—Kt1; 33 R—Kt1, Kt—K3; 34 B—K3, Kt—B2; 35 B—B1, or 32 . . ., R—R1 (to answer R—Kt1 with Q×Rch.); 33 P—Kt3, Kt—K3; 34 B—K3, Kt—B2; 35 K—Kt2, Kt—Kt4; 36 R—QKt1. He therefore tries another tack, to which White finds another neat answer.

32.	Q×P	P×B

Forced, if he is not to remain a piece down.

33.	Q×Q	R—Kt1
34.	P—Q5	

If R—Kt1, then 34 . . ., P—Kt4 cutting off the bishop and threatening P—B8=Qch. But White is out of the wood now and actually a pawn ahead.

34.		P—Kt8=Q
35.	Q—B4	Kt—Kt2
36.	P—K6	

But this attempt to exploit his advantage is premature and loses the pawn at once. Something like R—B1 first is indicated.

36.		P×P
37.	P×P	Q—Kt6
38.	Q—B7	Kt×P

A violent battle has ended in equality. By rights the analyst should be able to draw a line and write " Drawn," but White with stubborn obstinacy persists tediously in trying to pursue the vanished win and, as so often happens, makes a slip and loses. The game continued 39 Q—K7, Q—Q4; 40 P—KR4, Q—B3; 41 R—K1, R—K1; 42 Q—R3, R—Q1; 43 Q—QKt3, K—B2; 44 B—K3, R—QB1; 45 B—B1, Q—B5; 46 Q—B3ch., K—Kt1; 47 Q—

KB6, Kt—Kt2 ; 48 B—Kt2, Q—KB2 ; 49 Q—Q4, P—R4 ; 50 R—QB1, K—R2 ; 51 Q—Q3, Q—B4 ; 52 Q—Q4, Q—B2 ; 53 Q—K5, Q—B2 ; 54 Q—B6, R—Q1 ; 55 Q—KB3, Kt—B4 ; 56 Q—K2, R—QB1 ; 57 P—Kt3. And here is the slip though it is not necessarily fatal.

57. Kt×KtP
58. Q—Q3

Best was P×Kt, Q—Kt3ch. ; 59 K—Kt2, Q×B ; and Black can hardly hope to win. Now White must lose a second pawn.

58. Kt—B4
59. Q—K4 Q—QB5
60. Q—Kt7ch. R—B2
61. Q—Kt8

White is still fighting and now threatens mate.

61. Q—Kt5ch.
62. K—R1

If K—B1, then Q—Q8ch. ; 63 K—Kt2, with the same position as after the 65th move in the game.

62. Q×Pch.
63. K—Kt2 Q—Kt5ch.
64. K—R1

If K—R2, Q—B5ch. ; 65 K—Kt1, Kt—Kt2 ; 66 K—Kt2, R—B2 ; 67 Q—Kt6, Kt—B4 ; winning.

64. Q—Q8ch.
65. K—Kt2 Kt—R5ch.
66. K—R2

Playing the king to the 3rd rank would allow mate in two.

66. Q—Q3ch.
67. K—Kt1 Kt—B6ch.
68. K—B1

Now if K—Kt2, Q—R7ch. ; 69 K—B1 (K×Kt, R—B2ch. ; and wins), Kt—Q7ch. ; 70 K moves, R—K2ch. ; winning.

68. Q—R3ch.
69. K—Kt2 Kt—R5ch.
70. K—R2 Q—B1

After this, which breaks White's mating threat, positional and material superiority must tell.

71. Q—Kt6 Kt—B6ch.
72. K—Kt2 Q—Kt5ch.
73. K—B1 R—K2
Resigns.

G. H. Mackenzie (1837–1891) was a Scotsman who in 1863 emigrated to New York and became an American citizen. He was an exceptionally brilliant player and besides being American champion for many years, frequently played in European master tournaments. His best results were 1st at Frankfort, 1887 and 2nd at Bradford, 1888.

A. Burn (1848–1925) was one of the finest of all British masters, though his quiet unobtrusive style caused him to be overshadowed in the public imagination. Between 1870 and 1887 he only played in England, but scored a continuous run of first prizes. Afterwards competing abroad also he was strikingly successful, his best results being 1st prizes at Amsterdam, 1889, and Cologne, 1898, and 2nd at Breslau, 1889.

GAME 11

BURN–MACKENZIE

4th match game, London, 1886.

QUEEN'S PAWN GAME

1.	Kt—KB3	P—Q4
2.	P—Q4	Kt—KB3
3.	P—K3	P—K3
4.	P—QKt3	P—B4
5.	B—Kt2	Kt—B3
6.	QKt—Q2	P×P
7.	P×P	B—Q3
8.	B—Q3	B—Q2
9.	O—O	R—QB1
10.	P—B4	O—O
11.	R—K1	Kt—K2
12.	P—B5	B—Kt1
13.	P—QKt4	Kt—Kt3
14.	P—QR4	Kt—B5

In view of White's decision to play on his Q side majority, Black seeks to provoke a target for his own attack on the other wing.

15.	B—KB1	P—KR3
16.	P—Kt5	Kt—R2
17.	P—Kt3	

He has no objection to falling in with Black's plan since his white squares can be protected by his bishop, and the Black knight's retreat will allow White to enforce a weakened Black KP.

17.		Kt—Kt3
18.	B—Q3	P—B4
19.	R—K2	

In order to play P—B4.

19.		Kt—B3
20.	Kt—K1	Kt—K5
21.	P—B4	

[Diagram 15]

21.		B×BP

So far White has had decidedly the best of it and is now ready to resume his Q side operations. Black must there-

(BLACK) MACKENZIE

(WHITE) BURN

Position before Black's 21st move.

(DIAGRAM 15)

fore adopt fighting tactics if he is to have any counter-chances.

22.	P×B	Kt×KBP
23.	Kt(2)—B3	

If R—K3, Q—Kt4ch.; 24 K—B1 (K—R1, Kt—B7 Mate), Q—R5; 25 R—B3, Q×P (threatening Q—R8 Mate); 26 B×Kt, BP×B; with a tremendous attack.

23.		Kt×Rch.
24.	Q×Kt	B—K1
25.	B—B1	

To prevent Q—Kt4ch., in reply to his intended Kt—K5.

25.		P—Kt4
26.	Kt—K5	Q—B3
27.	R—R3	

A possible line for Black is 27 . . ., Kt—B6; 28 Q—QB2, R×P; 29 P×R, Q×Kt; 30 Kt—Kt2, Kt—K7ch.; 1 B×Kt, Q×R; and though some preparatory moves to strengthen Black's game may be preferable first, the mere possibility of such a variation indicates the value of this move by White. In addition it is the easiest way of bringing the rook to the defence of the other wing if it is required.

27.		K—R2
28.	B—B2	R—KKt1
29.	Kt—Kt2	R—Kt2
30.	B—Kt2	P—KR4
31.	P—R5	P—R5
32.	Kt—K3	

So that if 33 P—R6, P×P; then 34 R×P, threatening Kt×QP.

32.		K—Kt1
33.	P—R6	P—Kt5
34.	P×P	R×KtP
35.	B—Q3	Kt—Kt4
36.	R—R6	

Even better was 36 Q—B1, and after Kt—R6ch.; Black cannot play Kt—B5. The game now becomes most exciting.

36.		Kt—R6ch.
37.	K—R1	Kt—B5
38.	Q—Q2	Kt×B
39.	Kt×QP	

Just in time. After 39 Q×Kt, B×P; 40 Kt×QP, B×Q; 41 Kt×Qch., K—Kt2; 42 Kt×B, K×Kt; Black gets a good game.

39.		Q—Kt2

Not Q—Q1; 40 R—Q6, B—

Q2 ; 41 Kt×B, R×Kt (P×Kt; 42 Kt—B6ch.) ; 42 R×R, Q×R ; 43 Kt—B6ch.

(BLACK) MACKENZIE

(WHITE) BURN

Position before White's 40th move.

(DIAGRAM 16)

40. R×KP

Another fine move, giving up a piece to carry on the attack. B×P is now prevented by the threat of R—KKt6.

40. Kt×Kt
41. Kt—B6ch. K—B2

If K—B1 ; 42 P×Kt, B×P ; 43 Q—Q6ch., K—B2 ; 44 Q—Q5, transposing back into the game.

42. P×Kt B×P

Not K×R ; 43 Q—Q5ch., K—K2 ; 44 Q×Rch., K—B1 ; 45 Q×R, winning.

43. Q—Q5 K—B1
44. P—B6 Q—Kt4

Defence is no longer to be considered, and counter-attack is his only chance. The text move threatens Q—K6—K8ch., followed by P—R6 Mate.

45. R—K8ch.

Not 45 P×R, R—B8ch. ; 46 K—Kt2 (B×R, Q×Bch.; 47 K—Kt2, Q—B8 Mate), P—R6ch. ; 47 K—Kt3, P—B5ch. ; or 47 K—B2, Q—B5ch.

45. R×R
46. B—R3ch

Missing his chance. P×R can now be played for if Q—K6 ; 47 Q—Kt8ch., K—K2 ; 48 Kt—Q5ch., K—Q2 (K—Q1 ; 49 Kt×Q, R×Q; 50 P—Kt8=Qch.) ; 49 Q—B7ch., K—B3 ; 50 Kt×Q, wins easily. Or else 46 . . ., Q×Kt ; 47 B—R3ch., K—Kt2 ; 48 P×Qch., but not 47 P×Q, R—K8ch. ; 48 K—Kt2, R—K7ch. ; 49 K—B1, R—K4 dis.ch. ; 50 K—B2, R—K7ch. ; drawing.

46. K—Kt2
47. Kt×Rch. K—R1
48. P×R Q—K6

Black has taken a long chance and it has come off. White's reply is forced, for if 49 Q—Kt2, Q—K8ch. ; 50 Q—Kt1, B—B3ch.

49. B—B5 Q—B8ch.
50. B—Kt1 B—B3
51. Kt—B6

He has no time now to queen his pawn. A grand fight, even if Black was lucky.

51. B×Qch.
52. Kt×B Q—Kt8
Resigns.

I. Gunsberg (1845–1930), a Hungarian, spent almost all his chessplaying life in England. His tournament successes, which included firsts at Hamburg, 1885, and at London, 1888, secured his recognition as a contender for Steinitz's world title. Unsuccessful in this, he concentrated on chess journalism and practically retired from serious play.

S. Tarrasch (1862–1934), for all his failure to win the world title from his compatriot Lasker, remains one of the greatest of all chessplayers. His tournament record from 1884 to 1914 is studded with prizes and even to an advanced age he remained a dangerous competitor in International tournaments. His style, based on that of Steinitz, was simpler and more logical, if less imaginative, while his crystallisation of Steinitz's theories into precise dogmas made him one of the greatest of chess teachers and profoundly influenced the strategical appreciation of later players.

GAME 12

TARRASCH–GUNSBERG

Frankfort tournament, 1887.

FRENCH DEFENCE

1. P—K4 P—K3
2. P—Q4 P—Q4
3. Kt—QB3 P×P
4. Kt×P Kt—KB3
5. B—Q3

More usual is Kt×Ktch.

5. QKt—Q2
6. B—K3 Kt×Kt
7. B×Kt Kt—B3
8. B—Q3 B—Q2

The best development of this bishop is on QKt2, and though an immediate P—QKt3 would have been answered by 9 Q—B3, he would have been better advised to try 8 . . ., B—K2; 9 Kt—B3, P—QKt3. Now the bishop is condemned to a defensive role at best.

9. Kt—B3 B—Q3
10. O—O Kt—Kt5

A premature attempt to create weaknesses in White's position. After White's reply he had nothing better than 11 . . ., B—K2.

11. B—KKt5 P—KB3
12. B—Q2 Q—K2
13. P—KR3 Kt—R3
14. P—B4

Threatening P—B5.

14. P—B3
15. P—QKt4

Now he is in a position to attack Black on whichever side he castles, for 15 . . ., O—O would be answered by 16 B×

Kt. Black must castle into trouble, for he cannot play 15 . . ., B×P; to which Tarrasch gives the answer as 16 B×B, Q×B; 17 R—Kt1, Q—Q3; 18 R×P, O—O; 19 Q—B2, P—KB4; 20 P—B5, Q—Q4; 21 B—B4, Q—K5; 22 Q—B1, B—B1; 23 R—QB7, P—B5; 24 R—K1, Q—Kt3; 25 R×B, QR×R; 26 R×P, winning. A long but convincing analysis.

15.		O—O—O
16.	R—K1	B×P
17.	R—Kt1	B×B
18.	Q×B	K—Kt1

So as to defend the QKtP with the bishop, the threat otherwise being 19 Q—Kt2, B—K1; 20 R×P.

19.	P—B5	B—B1
20.	R—Kt3	Q—QB2
21.	KR—Kt1	K—R1
22.	R—Kt6	

The attack becomes fierce and brilliant. If now 22 . . ., P×R; 23 P×P, Q—Q3; 24 Q—R5ch., and mates. Less strong was 22 B—R6, R—Q2; but not 22 . . ., P×B; 23 Q—R5, Q—B5; 24 P—Kt3, and Black must give up his queen to prevent mate on his QKt1.

22.		P—K4
23.	R(1)—Kt4	KR—K1

Beginning counter-action in the centre just in time; the threat is P—K5, and it now becomes a race between White's attempts to break through on the wing and Black's to break through in the centre. 23 . . ., P×R; would still be fatal because of 24 P×P, Q—Q3; 25 R—R4ch., K—Kt1; 26 R—R8ch., K×R; 27 Q—R5ch.

24.	P×P	P×P

(BLACK) GUNSBERG

(WHITE) TARRASCH

Position before White's 25th move.

(DIAGRAM 17)

25.	R—QR4	P—K5
26.	Q—R5	Q—Kt1
27.	B×P	B—B4

The culmination of Black's counter-play; all his pieces come to life and White cannot move the bishop because of 28 . . ., R—Q8ch.; 29 Kt—K1, R(8) × Ktch. Nevertheless, better was 27 . . ., R—Q8ch.; 28 Kt—K1, Kt—B4.

28.	R—R6

Attack and counter-attack continue in delicate balance.

Now White threatens mate in two and if 28 . . ., P×R; 29 B×Pch.

28. R—Q8ch.
29. Kt—K1 R×Ktch.

Apparently turning the tide in his favour, but White is not finished yet.

30. Q×R B×B
31. R×B

The saving clause. 31 R×Pch., Q×R; 32 R×Qch., K×R; 33 P—B3, B—Kt3; 34 Q—R5ch., would leave him very problematical drawing chances. The text gives up a piece but wins the game.

31. R×R
32. Q×R P×R
33. Q×Pch. Q—Kt2
34. Q—K8ch. Q—Kt1
35. Q—K4ch. Q—Kt2
36. P—B6

The key to his 31st move.

36. Q—QB2
37. Q—K8ch. Q—Kt1
38. Q—Q7 Q—Kt8ch.

There is no longer any defence to the threat of P—B7.

39. K—R2 Kt—B4
40. P—B7 Resigns.

J. H. Blackburne (1841–1924) was the greatest of all British tournament players, and so dangerous that he was known as "The Black Death." No great player ever had a career at once so successful and so long; his first International tournament was London, 1862, and in his last, at St. Petersburg in 1914, he won a brilliancy prize. His brilliant, ingenious style was unsuited to match play; among his best tournament results were 1st prizes at London, 1876, Berlin, 1881, Hereford, 1885, equal 1st prizes at Vienna, 1873, Weisbaden, 1880, London, 1886, and 2nd prizes at London, 1872, Nuremburg, 1883, and Manchester, 1890.

GAME 13

MACKENZIE–BLACKBURNE

Bradford tournament, 1888.

Queen's Pawn Game

1. Kt—KB3 P—Q4
2. P—Q4 B—Kt5

Irregular but playable. There is nothing for White in 3 Kt—K5, B—R4.

3. P—K3 P—K3
4. B—K2 Kt—KB3
5. P—QKt3 P—B4
6. B—Kt2 Kt—B3
7. QKt—Q2 R—B1

Now Black is playing the Pillsbury Attack with the colours reversed.

8. O—O P×P
9. P×P B—Q3
10. P—B4 O—O
11. R—K1 P—KR3

But here he loses time. Better was Q—K2.

12. P—QR3 Kt—Q2
13. P—B5 B—B5
14. P—Kt4 P—KKt4

The point of his 11th move. But though the attack, especially in Blackburne's hands, may become dangerous, it creates a serious weakness on his K side, and White remains with a solid Q side pawn majority once the attack is broken.

15. Kt—B1 Q—B3
16. P—Kt3

This leads him into a very involved defence. Simpler was 16 P—R3, B—R4; 17 Kt (3) —R2.

16. B—Kt1
17. Kt—K3 P—KR4

An ingenious continuation, for if in reply 18 Kt×B then P×Kt; 19 Kt—Q2, Kt×QP; threatening Kt×Bch., or Kt—B6ch.

18. K—Kt2 Q—Kt2
19. Kt×B P×Kt
20. Kt—Kt1 P—B4
21. P—Kt5 Kt—Q1
22. R—Kt1

Black threatened 22 . . ., Kt×P; 23 P×Kt, Q×B.

22. Kt—KB3
23. P—B3 P×Pch.
24. Kt×P P—Kt5
25. Kt—R4 P—B5
26. B—Q3 Kt—R4
27. Kt—Kt6 P—B6ch.

The position is now most complicated and both players are going all out to win. Black is not content to force the draw by 27 . . ., P×P; 28 Kt×R, Kt—B5ch.; 29 K—Kt1 (K—R1, P—Kt7ch.; 30 K—Kt1, Q—R3; 31 Q×Pch., K×Kt; 32 B—B2, Kt—K7ch.; 33 R×Kt, Q×Pch.; wins), Kt—R6ch.; 30 K—Kt2, Kt—B5ch. Any attempt by White to sidetrack this variation fails, as for example 28 Q×P (P×P, R—B6), Kt—B5ch; 29 K—R1, P—Kt7ch.; 30 K—Kt1, Kt×B.

28. K—B2 R—KB3
29. Q—B2 P—Kt3

Black now wants to force White to play P—B6, for though this will give him a strong passed pawn, it blocks the Q side to any activity by the pieces.

30. QR—Q1 B—Q3
31. P—B6 Kt—B2
32. B—QB1 R—B2
33. P—QR4 B—Kt5

Preventing P—R5 and so keeping the Q side blocked.

34. R—R1 Kt—Q3

Now he returns to his K side attack with the idea ultimately of posting a knight on his K5.

35. Kt—K5 Kt—B4
36. B×Kt

Virtually forced, for if 36 B—Kt2, then Kt—R5; 37 P×Kt, P—Kt6ch.; 38 P×P, Q×Pch.; 39 K—B1, R—K Kt2; 40 P—B7, Q—Kt7ch.; 41 Q×Q, P×Q dbl.ch.; 42 K—Kt1, P×R=Qch.; 43 K×Q, R×P; winning.

36. R×B
37. Q—Q3 Kt—B3
38. B—B4 Kt—K5ch.
39. K—B1

(BLACK) BLACKBURNE

(WHITE) MACKENZIE

Position before Black's 39th move.

(DIAGRAM 18)

39. Q—R2

Though this threatens 40 . . ., Q—R6ch.; 41 K—Kt1, Q—Kt7 Mate, the square KR3 would be even stronger for the queen, and a better line was 39 . . ., R×B; 40 P×R, Q—R3; 41 P—R4, Kt—Kt6ch.; 42 K—B2, Kt×Rch.; 43 R×Kt, R—KKt2; 44 Q—Kt3 (P—B7, R×P; 45 Q—Kt6ch., Q×Q; 46 Kt×Q, R—B7ch.; wins), Q×BP; 45 Q×B, P—Kt6ch.; winning.

40. P—R4 R×B
41. P×R Kt—Kt6ch.
41. K—B2 Kt—K5ch.

He has sacrificed the exchange one move too late, for now after 42 . . ., Kt×Rch.; 43 R×Kt, he has nothing better than 43 . . ., Q—Kt2; 44 Q—Kt6, or 43 . . ., Q×Q; 44 Kt×Q, B—B6; 44 K—K3, holding everything.

43. K—K3 R—KKt2
44. P—KR5

Now White fights back against the dangerous passed pawns by threatening to force the rook off the Kt file.

44. B—Q3
45. P—R6 B×Kt

The persistence with which Black keeps up his attack is as remarkable as it is brilliant. Now if 46 P×R, B×BPch.; 47 K×B, Q—B4ch.; 48 K—K3, Q—Kt4 Mate.

46. QP×B R—KB2

Now the threat is Q—B4.

47. R—R5 P—Kt6

Making a last determined effort to win, whereas after the more natural P—B7 he could hardly lose; for example, 48 Q—K2, P—Kt6; 49 Q—Kt

4ch., K—R1; 50 R—QB1, Kt—B3; 51 P×Kt, Q—K5ch.; 52 K—Q2, P—Kt7; 53 P—B7, P—B8=Ktch.; 54 R×Kt, P×R=Ktch, or 48 Q—K2, Q—Kt3; 49 R(Q)—KR1, P—Kt6; 50 R(1)—R4, K—R2. As it turns out, the safer P—B 7 was a better line.

48. K×P R×Pch.

The point of his previous move. If in reply 49 K×R, then Q—B2ch.; 50 K—Kt4 (K—K3, Q—B7 Mate), Kt—B7ch.; 51 K×P, Kt×Q; winning.

49. K—Kt2 R—B7ch.
50. K—Kt1 Q—KB2
51. R—R4

Now White threatens to break the whole attack by 52 R×Kt, P×R; 53 Q×Pch. Black had no better reply than 51 . . ., R—B4; after which 52 R×Kt, P×R; 53 Q—Q8ch., K—R2; 54 P—B7, wins.

51. R—B6
52. P—R7ch. K—R1
53. P—B7

The passed pawn now comes in with devastating effect.

53. Q×BP
54. Q×R Q—B4ch.
55. K—R1 Q—KB7

Fighting to the bitter end, but the game is past saving now.

56. Q×Q Kt×Qch.
57. K—Kt2 Kt×R
58. K×P Resigns.

M. Weiss (1857–1927), during the few years in which he participated in master chess was a frequent prizewinner. His biggest success was in his last tournament when he tied for 1st prize at New York, 1889. He was a Hungarian.

M. I. Tchigorin (1850–1908) was the greatest Russian master of the second half of the nineteenth century. His aggressive unorthodoxy secured him many prizes, of which his tie for 1st prize at New York, 1889, was one of the most noteworthy. He unsuccessfully contested two matches with Steinitz for the world title.

GAME 14

WEISS–TCHIGORIN

New York tournament, 1889.

Tie Match, 1st game.

RUY LOPEZ

1. P—K4 P—K4
2. Kt—KB3 Kt—QB3
3. B—Kt5 P—QR3
4. B—R4 Kt—B3
5. Kt—B3 B—Kt5

Preferring to try for a transposition to the Four Knights Game rather than defend against the Ruy Lopez by P—QKt4 or P—Q3. However, he finds next move that he has to revert to the Ruy Lopez after all.

6. Kt—Q5 B—K2

For if Kt×P; 7 Q—K2, Kt—B3; 8 Kt×P, with a good game.

7. P—Q3 P—Q3
8. Kt×B Q×Kt
9. P—B3 P—R3
10. P—KR3 O—O
11. P—KKt4

This advance, indicating a determination to play for a win at all costs, is only possible because he has reserved the option of castling on the Q side.

11. Kt—KR2

To prevent P—Kt5. If 11 . . ., P—KKt4; 12 P—R4, B×P; 13 P×P, securing open files against Black's king.

12. R—KKt1 Kt—Q1
13. B—K3

Not so good now would be 13 P—Kt5, P—KR4; 14 P—Kt6, P×P; 15 R×P, B×P; 16 B—R6, Kt—K3; threatening B—Kt5.

13. Kt—K3
14. P—R4 P—KKt4

Forced at last, but White is now unable to derive any advantage from it.

15. P×P P×P
16. Q—K2 Q—B3

Preventing White from playing Q—B1—R3

17. O—O—O Kt—B5
18. B×Kt Q×Bch.
19. Kt—Q2

If 19 K—Kt1, B×P. Black has now managed to obtain the initiative, and in what appears to be a solid position he produces a series of tactical threats in order to reinforce and increase his advantage.

19. K—Kt2
20. P—B3 B—K3
21. B—Kt3 R—R1
22. R—R1 Kt—B3
23. K—Kt1 B—Q2

Threatening 24 . . ., Kt×KtP; 25 P×Kt, B×P; 26 Q—Kt2, B×R; which would at present be answered by 25 B×B.

24. R(Q)—Kt1 P—Kt4
25. Kt—B1 P—R4
26. P—R3 P—Kt5
27. BP×P P×P
28. R×R

Not 28 P×P, R—R8ch.; 29 K×R, Q—B8ch.; 30 K—R2, R—R1ch.; 31 B—R4, B—K3ch.; 32 P—Kt3, R×B Mate. White's position is now seen to be exceedingly precarious; he gains a pawn which is of little value and loses the KR file.

28. R×R
29. P×P R—R6
30. B—Q1 B—Kt4
31. Kt—K3 K—B1

Threatening 32 . . ., Kt×KP; 33 BP×Kt, R×Kt; which would at present be answered by 33 Kt—B5ch.

32.	Kt—B4	R—R7
33.	R—Kt2	R—R8
34.	K—B2	P—Q4
35.	Kt—R3	

Black is fighting all the time to establish an advantage. If now 35 P×P, Kt×P; 36 K—Kt3 (Q×P, Q×Q; 37 Kt×Q, Kt—K6ch.), B×Ktch.; 37 P×B, Kt—K6; 38 R—B2, R×B; winning.

35.		B—B3
36.	P—Kt5	B—Kt2
37.	R—B2	

The threat now was 37 . . ., P×P; 38 QP×P, Kt×KP; 39 P×Kt, B×Pch.; 40 K—Kt3, B×R; 41 Q×B, R×B; and wins.

37.		R—Kt8
38.	Q—Q2	Q—Kt6
39.	R—R2	P×P
40.	QP×P	

[Diagram 19]

40.		R×B

Now White had a threat of Q—Q8ch., followed by Q—R8ch. The text move is a fine attempt to force the win. If in reply 41 K×R then Q×Pch.; 42 R—K2 (K—B1, Q—B8ch.; 43 Q—Q1, Q—KB5ch.; 44 R—Q2, Kt×KP), B×P; 43 Q—Q8ch., K—Kt2; 44 Q×P, Kt×P; with a dangerous attack.

41.	R—R8ch.

(BLACK) TCHIGORIN

(WHITE) WEISS

Position before Black's 40th move.

(DIAGRAM 19)

A magnificent counter-attack which comes within an ace of winning.

41.		K—Kt2
42.	Q×Pch.	K×R
43.	Q×Ktch.	K—Kt1
44.	K×R	Q—B7

It is Black now who must fight for a draw, since he must come out a pawn down.

45.	Kt—B2	Q—B8ch.
46.	K—Q2	Q×KtP
47.	P—Kt4	B—R3
48.	Q—Q8ch.	K—R2
49.	Q×P	Q—Q6ch.
50.	K—B1	Q×BP
51.	Q×P	Q×KtP
52.	Q—B5ch.	

Even with the queens off, White cannot quite force a win.

52.		Q×Q
53.	P×Q	K—Kt2

54.	K—Q2	K—B3
55.	Kt—Q4	K—K4
56.	K—B3	P—B3

Drawn

For after 57 P—Kt5, B—Kt2 ; 58 K—B4, B—Q4ch ; 59 K—B5, B—R1 ; White can only advance his pawn with the help of his king or his knight, and the king is tied to the knight and the knight to the BP. A great game up to the very last situation.

H. N. Pillsbury (1872–1907), an American, was one of the greatest players of his time and his premature death was a tragic loss. He sprang to fame by winning the Hastings tournament, 1895, ahead of almost all the world's masters. His chess was marked by the will to win on all possible occasions.

GAME 15

PILLSBURY–TARRASCH

Hastings tournament, 1895.

PILLSBURY ATTACK

1.	P—Q4	P—Q4
2.	P—QB4	P—K3
3.	Kt—QB3	Kt—KB3
4.	B—Kt5	B—K2
5.	Kt—B3	QKt—Q2
6.	R—B1	O—O
7.	P—K3	P—QKt3
8.	P×P	P×P
9.	B—Q3	B—Kt2
10.	O—O	P—B4

Both players are on familiar ground, Pillsbury playing the variation of the Queen's Gambit Declined (4 B—Kt5) named after him, and Tarrasch playing for a queen side pawn majority, the advantage of which he was the first to propound as a theory.

11. R—K1

The subsequent course of the game suggests that this is loss of time.

11.		P—B5
12.	B—Kt1	P—QR3
13.	Kt—K5	P—Kt4
14.	P—B4	R—K1
15.	Q—B3	Kt—B1
16.	Kt—K2	Kt—K5
17.	B×B	R×B

With a view to doubling rooks.

18. B×Kt

A rather surprising move since it gives Black more freedom, but in return he secures the free use of his KKt3 and blocks any frontal attack on his weak KP.

18. P×B
19. Q—Kt3 P—B3

Safe enough now that White's KB is gone, and at the same time both driving White from his outpost and forestalling any attack by P—B5—B6.

20. Kt—Kt4 K—R1
21. P—B5 Q—Q2
22. R—B1 R—Q1

Black loses a little time with this rook. As he will soon have to defend his KP a third time, QR—K1 at once was better.

23. R—B4 Q—Q3
24. Q—R4 R(Q)—K1
25. Kt—Kt3 B—Q4

Threatening P—Kt5, which White only manages to delay for one move by threatening the KP.

26. Kt—B2 Q—B3
27. R—B1 P—Kt5
28. Kt—K2

The drama begins to develop. Against Black's threats on the Q side, White must bring back this knight to cover his QB1.

28. Q—R5
29. Kt—Kt4 Kt—Q2

Not yet Q×P because of 30 Kt×P, P×Kt; 31 Q×Pch., winning.

30. R(4)—B2 K—Kt1

And again not Q×P because of 31 Kt—B4, B—B2; 32 Kt—Kt6ch., B×Kt; 33 P×B, with a winning game; for example, 33 . . ., P—R3; 34 Kt×RP (threatening mate in two), P×Kt; 35 Q×Pch., K—Kt1; 36 R—B4, and 37 R—R4, or again 33 . . ., Kt—B1; 34 Kt×P, P×Kt (P—R3; 35 Kt×R, winning easily); 35 R×P, K—Kt1; 36 R—B7.

31. Kt—B1 P—B6

Now it is Black's turn again and he forces a dangerous passed pawn.

32. P—QKt3 Q—B3
33. P—KR3 P—QR4
34. Kt—R2 P—R5
35. P—Kt4 P×P
36. P×P R—R1

Considering that he has only to win White's QKtP to have an overwhelming game; yet there is such latent power in White's attack that P—R3 would be safer.

37. P—Kt5 R—R6
38. Kt—Kt4

[Diagram 20]

38. B×P

The correct line was to take the pawn with the rook, since after the exchange the bishop could return to the defence whereas the rook cannot. But Black is still underestimating White's chances.

39. R—KKt2

A threat again at last, though it seems to have come almost too late. The intention is to

(BLACK) TARRASCH

(WHITE) PILLSBURY

Position before Black's 38th move.

(DIAGRAM 20)

play 40 P×P, Kt×P; 41 Kt×Ktch.

39.		K—R1
40.	P×P	P×P

Not Kt×P; 41 Kt—K5, Q—K1; 42 Kt—Kt6ch.

41. Kt×B

The key to his plan. Black's piece on his QKt6 is to be virtually out of the game.

41.		R×Kt
42.	Kt—R6	R—Kt2

The only move against R—Kt8 Mate, for if R—K1; 43 Kt—B7 Mate.

43.	R×R	K×R
44.	Q—Kt3ch	K×Kt

He cannot play K—B1; 45 Q—Kt8ch., K—K2; 46 Q×R.

45.	K—R1	Q—Q4

Now he must prevent 46 R—KKt1 and 47 Q—R4 Mate.

46.	R—KKt1	Q×BP
47.	Q—R4ch.	Q—R4
48.	Q—B4ch.	Q—Kt4
49.	R×Q	P×R
50.	Q—Q6ch.	K—R4
51.	Q×Kt	P—B7

The last action of the hard won passed pawn is honourable hari-kari. This famous game is unequalled for the breathlessness of its split-second timing.

52. Q×P Mate

GAME 16

STEINITZ–PILLSBURY

St. Petersburg tournament, 1896.

PETROFF DEFENCE

1.	P—K4	P—K4
2.	Kt—KB3	Kt—KB3
3.	P—Q4	

Steinitz's own method of treating the Petroff Defence, introduced into master play for the first time in this game.

3.		P×P
4.	P—K5	Kt—K5
5.	Q—K2	

In another game against the same opponent in the same tournament Steinitz tried 5 Q×P, P—Q4; 6 P×P e.p.,

Kt×QP ; 7 B—Kt5, and again ultimately won.

5. B—Kt5ch.

Hoping to exchange his knight on his Q7, White being unable to play 6 P—B3 because of P×P ; 7 Q×Kt, P×P dis. ch. ; 8 Q×B, P×B=Qch.

6. K—Q1 P—Q4
7. P×P e.p. P—KB4
8. Kt—Kt5

Though this wins a piece by the threats of Q—B4 and P—KB3, Steinitz had previously condemned it as leading to a lost game.

8. O—O
9. Q—B4ch. K—R1
10. Q×B

A new discovery, previously not considered because of the answer Kt×Pch. The more obvious alternatives to the text move fail ; for example, 10 P×P, Kt×Pch. ; 11 K—K2, Q×K2ch. ; 12 K×Kt, Q—K8ch. ; 13 K—B3, Q×B ; threatening Q—K6 Mate, or 10 Kt×Kt, P×Kt ; 11 Q×B, Kt—B3 ; 12 Q—Q2, B—Kt5ch. ; 13 B—K2, R×P ; 14 R—K1, Q—B3 ; 15 P—B3, R×B ; 16 R×R, Q—B8ch.

10. Kt—QB3
11. Q—R3

After 11 Q—K1, Kt×Kt ; 12 P×P, Q—B3 ; 13 B×Kt, Q×B ; Black has the better game. Steinitz avoids this line by his veiled attack on the Black rook. Black must therefore accept the offer of the exchange as his best chance, and the game becomes intensely exciting.

11. Kt×Pch.
12. K—K1 Kt×R
13. P×P Q—K1ch.
14. B—K2 P—B5

Trying to bring all his pieces to bear by B—Kt5. Should White reply 15 P—R3, the cornered knight gets out.

15. K—B1 B—Q2
16. Kt—Q2 Kt—K4

Another attempt to extricate his knight by 17 . . ., Kt—Kt5 ; and if 18 B×Kt, B—Kt4ch. White cannot answer the text move with 17 K—Kt1 because of Kt—Kt5 ; 18 Q—KB3 (B×Kt, Q—K8ch. ; or K×Kt, Q×B), Q—K6ch. ; 19 Q×Q (K×Kt, Kt—B7ch. ; 20 K—Kt1, Kt—R6 dbl. ch. ; 21 K—B1, Kt×Kt), BP×Q ; 20 K×Kt, P×Kt ; with advantage.

17. Kt(2)—B3 Kt—Kt5
18. B—Q3

White has been forced to submit to the escape of the knight, so he prepares a counter-attack. The best reply was 18 . . ., P—KR3.

18. Kt(8)—B7
19. B×RP B—Kt4ch.

Underestimating White's resources and hoping to force the issue by his own attack. Correct was 19 . . ., Kt—B3 ; 20 B—B5, Kt(7)—Kt5.

20. K—Kt1 Q—K7

Threatening Q—Q8ch.

21. B—Q2

(BLACK) PILLSBURY

(WHITE) STEINITZ

Position before Black's 21st move.

(DIAGRAM 21)

21. Kt—Q8

Not quite sufficient is Kt—K6, threatening Kt—R6ch., because of 22 Kt—R4, defending the KKtP and threatening Kt—Kt6 Mate. White is suddenly seen to have no small counter-attack. The text move threatens Q—B8 Mate.

22. B—Q3 B×B

The attack is held, as the following variation shows: 22 . . ., Q—B7ch.; 23 K—R1, Kt(8)—K6; 24 B×Kt, Kt×B; 25 R—KKt1, B—B3; 26 Q—Q6, R—B3; 27 Kt—B7ch., R×Kt (not K—Kt1; 28 Q—Q8ch., R×Q; 29 P×R=Qch., K×Kt; 30 Kt—Kt5 Mate); 28 Q—Kt6, K—Kt1; 29 Q—R7ch., K—B1; 30 Q—R8ch., K—K2; 31 Q×R, B×Kt; 32 Q—Q8ch., K—K3; 33 P—B8=Qch., and wins. Black must therefore simplify in order to try and establish his material superiority.

23. Q×B Q×Q
24. P×Q Kt×KtP

This allows White to bring his rook to the support of his passed pawn, but if 24 . . ., Kt(8)—K6; 25 Kt—K6, obtaining at least material equality and a positional advantage.

25. R—Kt1 Kt×QP
26. R×P Kt—B4
27. R—Kt5 Kt—QR3
28. Kt—K6 R—B3

The battle continues unabated. If KR—B1; 29 R—R5ch., K—Kt1; 30 R—KKt5, Kt—K6; 31 R×Pch.

29. Kt(3)×P R—K1

R—QB1 at once would have saved a move. The text move prepares a not very dangerous trap.

30. R—R5ch. K—Kt1
31. R—KKt5

Which White avoids. An error would be 31 B×P, R×B; 32 Kt×R, R—K8 Mate.

31. Kt—K6
32. Kt×KtP R—QB1
33. Kt—K6 dis.ch. K—R1

If K—B2; 34 R—Kt7ch., K—K1; 35 R—Kt8ch., K—Q2; 36 R—Q8ch. But the position of the king on the edge of the board allows White to develop sharp mating threats.

34. B—R5 R—B2
35. Kt—K2 R—B4

White was threatening 36 B—B3ch., K—R2; 37 R—R5ch., K—Kt3; 38 Kt(2)×Pch., R×Kt; 39 Kt×Rch., K—B2; 40 R—R7ch., winning.

36. B—B3ch. K—R2
37. R—Kt7ch. K—R3
38. Kt(2)×P Kt×BP

Getting rid of the objectionable pawn at last, for if now 39 R×Kt, R×R; 40 Kt×R, R×Kt; and wins because of the threats of R—B8 Mate and R—B5. White, however, has a line to recover the exchange with a won ending.

39. R—Kt6ch. K—R2
40. Kt—Kt5ch. R×Kt
41. R×R Kt—K1
42. B—Q4 Kt—Q8
43. R—R5ch. K—Kt1
44. R—R8ch. K—B2
45. R—R7ch. K—Kt1
46. R—K7 R—Q1
47. Kt—K6 R—B1
48. P—KR4 Kt—B6
49. B×Kt

There is no need for further complications. The struggle, one of exceptional ferocity, is now over.

49. R×B
50. R×Ktch. K—B2
51. R—QR8 K×Kt
52. R×P K—B4
53. R—R4 R—B7
54. K—R2 R—Q7
55. K—R3 R—Q6ch.
56. P—Kt3 R—QB6
57. R—R5ch. K—Kt3
58. P—R4 R—B5
59. R—R6ch. K—R4
60. P—Kt4ch. Resigns.

For after 60 . . ., R×P; there follows 61 R—R6ch.

GAME 17

PILLSBURY–TCHIGORIN

St. Petersburg tournament, 1896.

TCHIGORIN DEFENCE

1. P—Q4 P—Q4
2. P—QB4 Kt—QB3

The Tchigorin Defence, which has not been regarded with great favour. If 3 Kt—QB3, P—K4.

3. Kt—KB3 B—Kt5
4. P—K3 P—K3
5. Kt—B3 B—Kt5
6. Q—Kt3 B×Kt
7. P×B KKt—K2
8. B—Q2 O—O
9. P—B4

If Black is allowed to play P—K4 he will have a very good game. After the text move he has to have recourse to a most eccentric development if he is to get any counter play.

9.		R—Kt1
10.	O—O—O	P×P
11.	B×P	P—QKt4
12.	B—Q3	

Not 12 B×KtP, B×Kt; 13 B×B, P—QR3; nor 12 Kt×P, B×Bch.; 13 R×B, P—QR3; losing a piece either way.

12.		B×Kt
13.	Q×B	R—Kt3

In order to play Kt—Q4.

14.	K—Kt1	P—QR4
15.	KR—Kt1	Kt—Kt5
16.	B—K4	Kt(2)—Q4
17.	Q—B5	Q—R1

Black's whole scheme of development is strikingly irregular, yet White has to treat it with the utmost respect. The threat now is Kt—B6ch., followed by Q×B with a well-posted queen and a considerable reduction in White's attacking chances. But at the cost of exchanging pieces White can now win a pawn.

18.	QB×Kt	P×B
19.	B×Kt	P×B
20.	Q×P(4)	R—QR3
21.	Q—Kt3	

The open QR file is good compensation to Black for his pawn. White dare not open the QKt file as well by 21 Q×P because of R—Kt1; 22 Q—K2, R×RP. Equally 21 P—QR3 will allow Black to open the QKt file by 21 . . ., R—R5; 22 Q—Q2, P—Kt5.

21.		R—Kt1
22.	R—Kt5	

Owing to the weakness of Black's QP, White is able to develop a counter-attack along his own open file without loss of time.

22.		P—QB3
23.	R(Q)—Kt1	P—Kt3
24.	P—B5	P—Kt5
25.	P×P	RP×P

It is now a critical race between the two attacks. Black threatens R—R6, but must first attend to his K side.

26.	Q—Q3	

White has emerged with the initiative. If Black replies R×P, then White breaks through with 27 R×Pch., K—B1; 28 R—Kt8ch., transposing into the actual game.

26.		K—B1

(BLACK) TCHIGORIN

(WHITE) PILLSBURY

Position before White's 27th move.

(DIAGRAM 22)

27. R×KtP R×P

He dare not play P×R because of 28 Q×P, R—R2 (R×P; 29 Q—B6ch., K—K1; 30 R—Kt8ch., K—Q2; 31 R—Kt 7ch. and mates); 29 Q—Kt8ch., K—K2; 30 Q—R7ch., K—K 3; 31 Q—R6ch., K—Q2(K—B4; 32 Q—Kt6 Mate); 32 R—Kt7ch., and mates.

28. R—Kt8ch. K—K2
29. R×R Q—R5

Black now seems to be in great trouble, having lost a whole rook. He has, however, this fighting reply which by its threat of R—R8 Mate ensures recovery of the piece.

30. R—Kt7ch. K—K3
31. K—B1

He has nothing better, for if he tries to lose the rook to his own advantage by 31 R—Kt 6ch., P—B3; 32 R×Pch., K×R; 33 K—B1, Black still has a mate by R—R8ch.; 34 K—Q2, Q—Q8 Mate.

31. R—R8ch.
32. K—Q2 R×R
33. Q—B2

If 33 Q—K2, Black answers Q—R8 threatening both Q×Pch. and Q—B8ch. Black will now recover the pawn with a drawn ending.

33. Q×Qch.
34. K×Q R—Kt7
35. R×KtP R×P
36. R—Kt7 R×Pch.
37. K—Q3 P—KB4

For some time White continues his efforts to win, but in vain. The game proceeded: 38 R—QB7, K—Q3; 39 R—B7, P—B4; 40 P×Pch., K×P; 41 R—B7ch., K—Q3; 42 R—B2, R—B6; 43 K—Q4, R—R6; 44 R—B2, K—K3; 45 P—Kt4, R—R5ch.; 46 R—B4, R—R8; 47 K—B5, R—B8ch.; 48 K—Q4 (not 48 K—Kt6, R—B6), R—QKt8; 49 K—B3, R—K8; 50 K—Q2, R—QR8; 51 K—Q3, R—R6ch.; 52 K—K2, K—K4; 53 R—Q4, R—Kt6; 54 R—KB4, R—B6; 55 K—Q2, R—B1; 56 K—Q3, R—B8; 57 K—Q2, R—QR8; 58 K—K2, R—R 7ch.; 59 K—Q3, R—KKt7; 60 K—B3, R—K7; 61 K—Q3, R—QR7; 62 K—B3. Drawn.

R. Charousek (1873–1899), was a Czech by birth but Hungarian by adoption. In a very brief career before he was overtaken by tuberculosis he showed himself a player of the very first rank, his most striking achievement being the winning of the Berlin, 1897 tournament.

GAME 18

CHAROUSEK–PILLSBURY

Nuremburg tournament, 1896.

FALKBEER COUNTER-GAMBIT

1. P—K4 P—K4
2. P—KB4 P—Q4
3. P×QP P—K5
4. P—Q3 Kt—KB3
5. P×P

A variation rendered suspect later and replaced by 5 Kt—Q2.

5. Kt×KP
6. Q—K2

The usual line is 6 Kt—KB3, B—QB4; 7 Q—K2, B—B4. Charousek is, however, leading to a new variation of his own on the 8th move, to which the best answer is 8 . . ., Kt—B3.

6. Q×P
7. Kt—Q2 P—KB4
8. P—KKt4 B—K2
9. B—Kt2 Q—R4
10. P×P Kt—KB3
11. Kt—B3 O—O
12. O—O Q—B4ch.

An indifferent method of defending the bishop. Kt—B3 at once was preferable.

13. K—R1 Kt—B3
14. Kt—Kt3 Q×KBP
15. KKt—Q4 Kt×Kt
16. Kt×Kt Q—B4

Had he omitted 12 . . ., Q—B4ch.; 13 K—R1, he could now play 16 . . ., B—B4; pinning the knight.

17. Kt—K6 B×Kt
18. Q×Bch. K—R1
19. B—K3 Q—Q3
20. Q—Kt3 P—B3
21. QR—Q1 Q—B2
22. B—Q2

In order to bring the queen over to the K side.

22. QR—K1
23. Q—Kt3 B—Q3
24. B—QB3 R—K2
25. Q—R4 Kt—Q4

Leading to situations of critical intensity in which he hopes to out-manœuvre his unknown opponent.

26. B×Kt P×B
27. Q—R5 B×P
28. Q×P

28 B—Kt4 is answered by R—K4; 29 Q—Kt4, Q×P (not R—Kt4; 30 Q×R); 30 Q—R3(R×B, R×R; 31 Q×R, Q×

Rch.), Q—K5ch.; or 29 Q—R4, P—Kt4; 30 Q—R3, R—K6; 31 Q—R5, R(B)—K1. After the text move, though there are no absolutely immediate threats, Black finds that his ingenuity may recoil upon himself, for danger is imminent owing to the pin of his bishop, to the pressure on the long diagonal and to the possibility in some eventualities of mate on the first rank.

28. R—KKt1
29. R—Q4 B—K4

Not B×P; 30 R—KR4, B—Kt6; 31 R×Pch., K×R; 32 Q—R5 Mate.

30. R—QB4

Preventing the exchange of bishops and threatening if 30 . . ., Q—Q3; 31 Q×Rch., K×Q; 32 R—QB8ch.

30. Q—Kt1
31. R—K1

In this critical situation Tarrasch suggested that White won by 31 R—K4, and the only lines which prevent White capturing the bishop are B—Q3; 32 R—KR4, B—K4; 33 R×Pch., K×R; 34 Q—K4ch., K—R3; 35 Q—R4ch., winning, or R—KB1; 32 R—Q1, B—Q3; 33 R—KR4, B—K4; 34 Q—K4 and 35 R—Q7, but in the latter variation J. H. White suggested 33 . . ., B—B5; holding everything, so Charousek's judgment appears to be upheld. P. W. Sergeant gives a fuller analysis in his collection of Charousek's games.

31. R—Q1

(BLACK) PILLSBURY

(WHITE) CHAROUSEK

Position before White's 32nd move.

(DIAGRAM 23)

To this White can no longer reply 32 B×B because the bishop would then be pinned on the rook, but apparently Black's move is still insufficient.

32. Q—B5

For, as G. W. Baines pointed out, White could now play 32 R×B, R×Q; 33 R×R(7), and there is no satisfactory answer to the four threats of B×Pch., R×KKtP, R(4)—B7 and R(4)—K4. His main analysis continues 33 . . ., R—Q8ch.; 34 K—Kt2, Q—Q1; 35 R(4)—K4, R—Q7ch.; 36 K—R3, Q—B1ch.; 37 K—Kt3, R—Q1; 38 R—KKt4, R—Kt1; 39 B—K5,

Q—B1; 40 R(7)×KKtP, with a winning ending.

32. B—Q3
33. R×R

The right idea just too late.

33. B×Q
34. R×KKtP

Not 34 R×B, Q—B5; 35 R ×KKtP, R—Q5.

34. R—Q8ch.
35. R—Kt1 dis.ch. B—Q5

The complications of defence with counter-attack on both sides constitute chess of the richest quality.

36. B×Bch. R×B
37. R×R

Now the two rooks are insufficient to win against the threat of perpetual check, though Charousek tries hard still to force the issue.

37. Q—KB1
38. R—Q3 Q—K2
39. P—KR3 P—KR4

Forestalling any chance of mate on his KKt1. White's attempts to get a rook onto the KR file with check are neatly foiled.

40. R(3)—KKt3 Q—K5ch.
41. R(1)—Kt2 Q—K8ch.
42. K—R2 Q—K4
43. P—KR4 Q—B5
44. K—Kt1 Q×P
45. P—B3 Q—KB5
46. R—Kt5 Q—K6ch.
47. K—R2 Q—B6
48. R(2)—Kt3 Q—K7ch.
49. K—R3 Q—K3ch.
50. K—R4 Q—K5ch.
Drawn.

For if 51 K×P, Q—R2ch.; 52 K—Kt4, Q—K5ch.; 53K—R3, Q—R8ch.

Dr. Em. Lasker (1868–1941) was world champion from 1894 to 1921 and through the whole of his playing career no master was ever more dangerous or more difficult to defeat. Yet he had no definable style ; he sought even at the cost of some temporary disadvantage to create a position where his skill could be given full play. His philosophy of the struggle to succeed by any means was applied by him to the chessboard as to life. He achieved a wonderful succession of tournament and match victories, among the greatest being his first prizes at St. Petersburg, 1914, and at New York, 1924.

GAME 19

STEINITZ–LASKER

5th match game, Moscow, 1896.

PILLSBURY ATTACK

1. P—Q4 P—Q4
2. P—QB4 P—K3
3. Kt—QB3 Kt—KB3
4. B—Kt5 B—K2
5. P—K3 O—O
6. Q—Kt3

A variation which has long since become obsolete.

6. P×P
7. B×P P—B4
8. P×P Q—R4
9. Kt—B3 Q×BP
10. O—O Kt—B3
11. B—Q3

The threat was Kt—QR4 winning a piece. 11 B—K2 looks more natural but White plans an attack along the diagonal.

11. Kt—QKt5
12. B×Kt P×B

Black cannot avoid the doubling of the pawns. If B×B ; 13 Kt—K4, Q—Kt3 ; 14 Kt×Bch., while if Kt×B ; 13 Kt—K4, Q—Q4 ; 14 Q×Q, P×Q ; 15 B×B, R—K1 ; 16 Kt—B6ch., P×Kt ; 17 B×P, winning a pawn.

13. B—Kt1

The natural continuation after his 11th move, although it shuts in the QR.

13. R—Q1
14. P—QR3 Kt—Q4
15. Q—B2 P—B4
16. Kt—Q4

Not P—KKt4 at once, for then Kt—B3.

16. B—B3
17. P—KKt4 Kt×Kt

After White's last violent attacking move, which also has obvious weaknesses, Black decides to play for a win. There is a clear draw by B×Kt ; 18 P×B, Q×P ; 19 P×P, Q—Kt5ch. ; 20 K—R1, Q—B6ch.

18. P×Kt P×P
19 Q×Pch. K—B1
20. B—K4

For all the constricting appearance of his 13th move, his QR is free for action before Black's even now.

20. K—K2

Threatening R—R1 winning the queen.

21. B—Kt6 R—B1
22. QR—Kt1 Q—KKt4

Now Black prepares to turn the opening of the K side to his own ends.

23. B—B2 R—R1
24. Q—K4 B—K4

Q—KR4 is answered by 25 Q—Kt2.

25. KR—Q1 B×Pch.
26. K—B1 P—B4

(BLACK) LASKER

(WHITE) STEINITZ

Position before White's 27th move.

(DIAGRAM 24)

Black misses the best move which is P—Kt3. If then 27 Kt—B6ch. (not Q×R, B—R3ch.), K—B1; 28 Q—Kt4ch., K—Kt2; 29 Q—Q4ch. (B—Q3, B—Kt2), P—K4; 30 Q—Q3, B—Kt2; with a pawn up and the better position.

27. R×Pch.

Seizing the opportunity to reassume the initiative with a fine sacrificial attack. Kt×Pch., suggested by some, does not seem to lead to such powerful continuations.

27. B×R

If 27 . . ., K—B1 (K—K1; 28 B—R4ch.); 28 Kt×Pch., K—Kt1 (B×Kt; 29 Q×B and mates); 29 R—Q8ch., Q×R; 30 R—Kt7 Mate. If 27 . . ., K—B3; 28 Q—B6, Q—Kt1 (B×R; 29 Q×B leads to the actual game); 29 Kt×KP, B×Kt; 30 R(1)—Q7, R—QB1; 31 Q—R6, R—B1; 32 B—Kt3.

28. Q×Bch. K—B3
29. Kt×KP

And now White in turn misses the best move which was 29 Kt×BP. If then P×Kt; 30 Q—B6ch., K—B2; 31 R—Q7ch. Or if 29 . . ., Q—Kt1; 30 Q—K7ch., K—Kt3 (K—K4; 31 Kt—Q6, R—QB1; 32 P—QB4, R×P; 33 Kt×R Mate); 31 Kt—Kt7 dis. ch., K—R3; 32 Q—B6 Mate. The best reply is 29 . . ., QR—K1; 30 R—Q7, Q—Kt1; 31 Kt—Kt7, R—Kt1; 32 Q—K4, R—R3; 33 Q×P, with a winning attack.

29. Q—Kt1

Not K×Kt; 30 B—Kt3ch., K—K4; 31 Q—Q5ch., K—B3; 32 Q—B7ch., K—K4; 33 Q—K6 Mate.

30. Kt—Q4

White's attack would die away after 30 Kt—B5, Q—B 5ch.; 31 Kt—Q3, or after 30 Kt—B7, B×Kt. He therefore plays for material compensation for his sacrifice.

30. R—Q1
31. B×P B—K4
32. B—K4

To free his queen from the need to guard his KR1, a plan which Black immediately counters.

32. Q—B5ch.
33. B—Q3 Q×P
34. Q—K4 B×Kt
35. P×B

Preferring to have the K file open before taking the checks.

35. Q×QP
36. Q—Kt6ch.

Now he has lost his material equality but again has sufficient positional compensation to secure the draw.

36. K—K2
37. R—K1ch. K—B1

If K—Q2 White draws by 38 Q—K6ch., K—B2; 39 R—B 1ch., K—Kt1; 40 R—Kt1ch., K—B2; 41 R—B1ch.

38. Q—B5ch. K—Kt1
39. Q—Kt6ch. K—B1
Drawn.

A fair ending to a game which both players tried to win, and which was all the keener for the failure always to find absolutely the best continuations.

GAME 20

LASKER–BLACKBURNE

London tournament, 1899.

Ruy Lopez

1. P—K4 P—K4
2. Kt—KB3 Kt—QB3
3. B—Kt5 P—Q3
4. P—Q4 B—Q2
5. P—Q5

A most unusual move, which relieves the tension in the centre but gives him a certain space advantage. His next move is the necessary corollary; otherwise Black frees his game with P—KB4.

5. Kt—Kt1
6. B—Q3 B—K2
7. Kt—B3 Kt—KB3
8. Kt—K2 P—B3
9. P—B4 Kt—R3
10. Kt—Kt3 Kt—B4
11. B—B2 P—QKt4

With a view to breaking the grip of the White pawns, but his pieces are not well posted for supporting the manœuvre and it recoils upon him.

12. P—Kt4 Kt—Kt2
13. QP×P B×P
14. P×P B×KtP
15. P—QR4 B—Q2
16. O—O P—Kt3

With a weak QP, and a Q side majority against him Black must try at all costs to get some sort of attack going.

17. P—R3 P—KR4
18. B—K3 P—R4
19. P—Kt5 R—QB1
20. R—B1 Kt—B4
21. Kt—Q2

Black was threatening P—R5 winning the KP. Now White threatens to open up new lines of attack by P—B4.

21. P—R5
22. Kt—K2 P—Kt4

Desperate situations call for desperate remedies, and Blackburne decides to sacrifice a pawn to hinder White's attack and further his own.

23. B×P R—KKt1
24. B×P B×RP
25. B—KKt3 B—K3
26. R—K1 Kt—Kt5
27. Kt—B1 B—Kt4
28. R—Kt1

Had White appreciated the full force of the attack which Black has conjured out of a lost position he would have played P—B4, though even then B—R5 gave Black a powerful offensive.

28. R—KR1
29. Kt—B3 B—KB5
30. Kt—Q5

If 30 B×B, Black plays Q—R5, though he also has 30 . . ., R—R8ch.; 31 K×R, Kt×Pch. The Black attack is now beginning to show in its true colours.

30. Q—Kt4
31. P—B3

Forced by the threat of Q—R4.

(BLACK) BLACKBURNE

(WHITE) LASKER

Position before Black's 31st move.

(DIAGRAM 25)

31. R—R8ch.

The brilliant culmination of a fighting recovery.

32. K×R B×B
33. Kt×B

If R—K2 (against Kt—B7 ch.), B—B7; 34 R×B (against Q—R5ch.), Kt×Rch.; 35 K—

Kt1, Kt×Q; with an advantage even more marked than that obtained in the actual game.

33. Kt—B7ch.
34. K—Kt1 Kt×Q
35. Kt—B5 B×Kt(B)
36. P×B Q—Q7

The game appears to be absolutely won, but it is White's turn now to fight back.

37. KR×Kt Q×B
38. QR—B1 Q×BP
39. Kt—Kt6 R—Q1
40. Kt—B4 Kt—Kt2
41. Kt—K3 Q—B5
42. K—B2 Q×P
43. R—B7 Kt—B4
44. R—KR1

Threatening mate on the move, a wonderful achievement after his hopeless position of eight moves earlier.

44. R—Q2
45. R—B8ch. K—K2
46. R(1)—R8

Making a last brave effort. If in reply 46 . . ., Q×P; White even now escapes with a draw by 47 R(B)—K8ch., K—B3; 48 Kt—Kt4ch., K—B4 (K—Kt4; 49 R(R)—Kt8ch.); 49 Kt—K3ch., K—B3 (K—B5; 50 P—Kt3ch., K—Kt4; 51 R(R)—Kt8ch.); 50 Kt—Kt4ch. A great game, Lasker's only loss in the tournament, and one which earned Blackburne the brilliancy prize.

46. Q—Q5

Resigns.

D. Janowski (1868–1927), a Pole by birth but French by adoption, was with Marshall regarded as the rising star of the beginning of the twentieth century. Eventually he achieved a match with Lasker for the world title, but was heavily defeated.

GAME 21

JANOWSKI–BURN

Paris tournament, 1900.

Ruy Lopez

1. P—K4 P—K4
2. Kt—KB3 Kt—QB3
3. B—Kt5 Kt—B3
4. O—O Kt×P
5. P—Q4 Kt—Q3
6. B—R4

An unusual move to which the best reply is P—K5. The normal variations are either 6 B×Kt, QP×B; 7 P×P, Kt—B4; 8 Q×Qch., or 6 P×P,

Kt×B; 7 P—QR4, P—Q3; 8 P—K6.

6. P×P
7. P—B3

A bold line by which he hopes to take advantage of the poor position of the Black knights. If Black replies P×P then 8 Kt×P, B—K2; 9 Kt—Q5, O—O; 10 B—B4, pinning the knight on the weak QBP. Black prefers to return one pawn.

7. B—K2
8. P×P P—QKt4

An elaborate but ultimately effective freeing manœuvre.

9. B—Kt3 Kt—R4
10. B—B2 B—Kt2
11. Kt—K5 O—O
12. Kt—QB3

Again temporarily fixing Black's KKt. If 12 . . ., P—Kt5; 13 Kt—R4, Kt(3)—B5; 14 Kt×Kt, Kt×Kt; 15 Q—Q3, wins. The move chosen by Black loses the QKtP and 12 . . ., P—QR3; was more solid.

12. Kt(4)—B5
13. P—QKt3 Kt—Kt3
14. Kt×KtP Kt×Kt
15. Q—Q3 P—KB4
16. Q×Kt P—QR4

Threatening B—R3.

17. Q—K2 B—Q4
18. R—K1 B—Kt5

With a few rapid strokes Black completes his development but comes out with yet another indefensible QKtP.

19. B—Q2 Q—R5
20. B×B P×B
21. Q—Q2 P—Q3
22. Kt—Q3 P—B5

Assuming the initiative. The threat of P—B6 prevents White from taking the QKtP.

23. P—B3 R—B4
24. Q—B2

And now not 24 Kt×KtP, R—KR4; 25 P—KR3, B×BP; 26 P×B, Q×P; with a winning attack.

24. Q—R3
25. Kt×KtP R—KR4
26. P—KR3 R—KB1
27. P—QR4

Threatening P—R5 winning a piece. 27 Kt×B would not be good because the Black knight would settle on his K6.

27. B—K3
28. P—R5

(BLACK) BURN

(WHITE) JANOWSKI

Position before Black's 28th move.

(DIAGRAM 26)

28. B×RP

Getting in the first blow in a very critical position and threatening R—Kt4. Any less vigorous line to save the knight would allow White's QRP to become a menace. If now 29 P×B, R×P; and wins.

29. P×Kt P×P
30. B—Q3

Too late to defend his KKt2.

30. B×P
31. Q×B

The queen cannot be saved, so he plays to get three pieces for it.

31. R—KKt4
32. R—R2 R×Qch.
33. R×R Q—B3
34. Kt—B6

Black's attack is over and now it is White who has the initiative again. He now threatens 35 Kt—K7ch., K—R1; 36 Kt—Kt6ch., P×Kt; 37 R—R2ch., K—Kt1; 38 B—B4ch.

34. P—Q4
35. Kt—K7ch. K—B2

Not K—R1; 36 B×P (threatening Kt—Kt6ch.), Q×Pch.; 37 K—R1, R—R1; 38 R—KR2.

36. R—K5 P—Kt3
37. Kt×QP Q—Q1
38. R—K7ch. K—Kt1
39. B—B4

Playing for a win. He could force a draw by 39 B×P, P×B; 40 R×Pch., K—R1; 41 R—R6ch., K—Kt1; but any attempt to continue this variation for a win leads nowhere; for example, 42 R(6)—R7, R—B2; 43 R(K)×R, Q×Kt; 44 R(B)—Kt7ch., K—B1; 45 R—Q7, Q—Kt4ch.; 46 K—B1, Q—Kt4ch.; 47 K—B2, K—Kt1; 48 R(Q)—Kt7ch., K—B1; 49 R—R7, K—Kt1; 50 R (KR)—Kt7, Q—K1.

39. K—R1
40. R—KR2 P—KR4
41. R—K6 R—B4

Better than K—Kt2 or R2; 42 R—KKt2. Black now threatens to break the attack by R×Kt.

42. R(R)—K2 K—R2
43. R—K7ch. K—R3
44. R—K8 Q—R5
45. R—KKt2 P—QKt4

(BLACK) BURN

(WHITE) JANOWSKI

Position before White's 46th move.

(DIAGRAM 27)

Apparently succeeding at last in breaking up White's game with advantage, but White finds a brilliant continuation to the attack.

46. R—R8ch. K—Kt2
47. R—Kt8ch.

The point. Black cannot reply 47 . . ., K×R ; because of 48 Kt—K7 dbl. ch., K—R2 (K—Kt2 ; 49 Kt×Rch., or K—B1 ; 49 Kt×Pch.) ; 49 B—Kt8ch., K—R3 ; 50 R×P Mate.

47. K—B2
48. R(2)×P P×B

Black dare not try 48 . . ., Q—K8ch. ; 49 K—R2, Q—B7ch. ; 50 R—Kt2, Q×QP ; 51 R(2)—Kt7ch., K—K3 ; 52 R—K7ch., K—Q3 ; 53 R—Q8ch., K—B4 ; 54 R—B7 Mate. After the text move White must take the draw.

49. R(8)—Kt7ch.

For now 49 R(6)—Kt7ch., fails because the king can take the knight.

49. K—K1
50. R—Kt8ch. K—B2

If R—B1 ; 51 Kt—B7ch., K—Q2(K—B2 ; 52 R(8)—Kt7 Mate, or K—K2 ; 52 Kt—Q5ch., or K—Q1 ; 52 Kt—K6ch) ; 52 R(6)—Kt7ch., K—B3 ; 53 R×R. A tremendous game.

51. R(8)—Kt7ch. K—B1
52. R—Kt8ch. K—B2

Drawn.

F. J. Marshall (1877–1944) was the brilliant young American master who burst upon the chess world early in the twentieth century with great tournament victories such as those at Cambridge Springs, 1904, and Nuremburg, 1906. A certain unsoundness was compensated by exceptional ingenuity and this earned him a reputation as the originator of the famous Marshall "swindles." In matches he was not successful, being heavily defeated both by Lasker and by Capablanca. G. Marco was a prominent Austrian master.

GAME 22

MARSHALL–MARCO

Monte Carlo tournament, 1904.

SCOTCH GAMBIT

1. P—K4 P—K4
2. Kt—KB3 Kt—QB3
3. P—Q4 P×P

4. B—QB4 B—B4
5. P—B3 P—Q6

P×P had been known for more than half a century to give White a dangerous attack. For example, 5 . . ., P×P; 6 Kt×P, P—Q3; 7 O—O, Kt—B3; 8 B—KKt5, B—K3; 9 Kt—Q5, B×Kt; 10 P×B, was a consultation game Saint-Amant and Horwitz—Staunton and Harrwitz, Hull, 1847, or 7 . . ., B—K3; 8 B×B, P×B; 9 Q—Kt3, Q—B1; 10 B—K3, a match game, Staunton—Jaenisch, 1851. After the text move White cannot easily develop the QKt. Compare Game 8.

6. O—O P—Q3
7. Q×P

P—QKt4, B—Kt3; 8 Q—Kt3, to hinder Black's castling came into consideration.

7. Kt—B3
8. P—QKt4 B—Kt3
9. P—QR4 P—QR3
10. R—K1

Better was 10 B—KKt5. Marshall probably wanted to retain the option of playing B—R3 and P—K5.

10. Kt—Kt5
11. R—R2 Kt(5)—K4
12. Kt×Kt Kt×Kt
13. Q—Kt3

The inferiority of his 10th move is now clear. P—K5 is prevented and if 13 Q—K2, then 13 . . ., Kt×B; 14 Q×Kt, B—K3; winning the exchange. Marshall must therefore counter-attack at all costs.

13. Kt×B
14. Q×KtP R—B1
15. P—K5

It is not sufficient to get a rook for two bishops by 15 B—R6, Q—K2; 16 Q×P, B—K3; 17 B×R, Q×B.

15. Kt×P

Better was P×P; 16 R(2)—K2, B—K3; 17 B—R6, Q—K2.

16. K—R1

Threatening P—KB4 recovering the piece.

16. B—K3
17. R(2)—K2

The rapid doubling of the rooks has the surprise effect of recovering the piece, for he threatens P—KB4—B5 as well as 18 P—KB4, Kt—Q6; 19 R×Bch., P×R; 20 R×Pch., and mates.

17. Q—K2
18. P—KB4 Kt—Q6

[Diagram 28]

19. P—B5

A most interesting situation. 19 . . ., Kt×R; 20 R×Kt, B—B7; 21 B—Kt5, with a fearful grip on Black's game as for example after 21 . . ., Q—Q2; 22 R—K2, B—Kt3; 23 Q—B6, R—KKt1; 24 P×B, P×P; 25 R×Pch., nor can Black try 19 . . ., Kt×B; 20 R×Kt (bad would be R×B, P×R; 21 R×P, Q×R; 22

(BLACK) MARCO

(WHITE) MARSHALL

Position before White's 19th move.

(DIAGRAM 28)

P×Q, R—B8 Mate), O—O—O ; 21 P×B, with any effect. He can however play 19 . . ., Kt× R ; 20 R×Kt, and now O—O—O ; 21 B—Kt5, Q—Q2 ; 22 B×R, R×B ; 23 P×B, P×P ; with a slightly better game than he actually gets.

19.		Kt—K4
20.	P×B	P×P
21.	B—R6	Q×Q
22.	B×Q	R—B4
23.	B×Kt	R×B
24.	R×R	P×R
25.	P—Kt3	

The pawn cannot be defended and if R×P at once, 25. . ., R—Q1 ; forces the rook back to the first rank.

25.		R—Q1
26.	K—Kt2	R—Q6
27.	R×P	K—B2
28.	R—K2	B—K6

Preventing R—Q2 by White. He is now content to draw, but Marshall has other ideas and the complex developments which he conjures out of this simple position are an object lesson in fighting chess.

29.	R—B2	B—R3
30.	R—B2ch.	K—K2
31.	R—B3	R—Q8
32.	R—B1	R—Q6
33.	R—B3	R—Q8
34.	Kt—R3	

The only move if he is to play for a win, but it costs him his QRP.

34.		R—QB8
35.	P—B4	R—QR8
36.	P—B5	B—B8
37.	Kt—B4	R×P
38.	Kt—K5	B—Kt7

If R×P ; 39 R—B7ch., K—Q1 ; 40 R—Q7ch., K—B1 ; 41 R×P, threatening R—R8 Mate.

39.	Kt—Q3	B—B6
40.	R—B4	P—QR4
41.	R—R4	P×P
42.	R×Pch.	K—Q1
43.	Kt—B4	P—Kt6
44.	Kt×Pch.	K—B1
45.	P—B6	

[Diagram 29]

Now White has landed himself in serious trouble and has no prospect of stopping the QKtP after R×Pch. The text move is not quite sound but the fact that it succeeds shows how effectively Marshall has brought the game into a state of crisis.

(BLACK) MARCO

(WHITE) MARSHALL

Position before Black's 45th move.

(DIAGRAM 29)

45. B—K4

Black sees that the QKtP is now brilliantly stopped after 45 . . ., P×P; 46 R×Pch., K—Kt1; 47 R—Kt7ch., K×R; 48 Kt—B5ch., K—Kt3; 49 Kt×Rch., K—Kt4; 50 Kt×Bch., K—Kt5; 51 Kt—Kt1, P—Kt7; 52 P—R4, P—B4; drawing, and a drawing line no longer suits him. There was, however, a win in the above variation, had he seen it, by 48 . . ., K—R2; 49 Kt×R, B—Q5 (B—R1; 50 P—R4, K—R3; 51 Kt—B5ch.); 50 K—B3, K—R3; 51 K—K4, K—R4; 52 K×B, K×Kt; and the QKtP goes home. The text move which looks secure enough gives Marshall just the chance for which he has been struggling.

46. P×Pch. K—Kt1
47. Kt—B5 R—R7ch.
48. K—R3 P—Kt7
49. R—K7

A fine move. If in reply 49 . . ., P—Kt8=Q; 50 R—K8ch, K—R2; 51 R—R8ch., K—Kt3; 52 P—Kt8=Qch., K×Kt; 53 Q×Q, winning.

49. K—R2
50. R—K8 P—B3

By covering White's queening square Black seems to have assured the successful queening of his own pawn, but White has worked out one of the brilliant combinations which became known as "Marshall's swindles."

51. R—R8ch. K—Kt3
52. R×R P—Kt8=Q
53. P—Kt8=Qch. B×Q
54. R—Kt2ch. Q×R
55. Kt—R4ch. K—Kt4
56. Kt×Q P—B4
57. K—Kt2

And now the end game starts all over again with White a pawn to the good, but a great deal of equality still in the position. If 57 P—Kt4, P—B5; 58 P—Kt5, P—B6; 59 Kt—Q3, K—B5; 60 Kt—K1 (Kt—B1, B—B5), K—Q4; 61 K—Kt4, B×P; draws.

57. P—B5
58. K—B3

If 58 Kt×P, K×Kt; 59 P—Kt4, and the Black king crosses in time to stop the pawns. For example, 59 . . ., K—Q4; 60 P—R4, K—K3; 61 K—B3, B—Q3; 62 K—K4,

B—K2; 63 P—Kt5, K—B2; 64 K—B5, K—Kt2; 65 P—R 5, B×P.

58. P—B6
59. Kt—Q3 K—B5
60. Kt—K1

Not 60 Kt—B1, B—Q3; with the threat of B—R6.

60. K—Q4

Now if 60 . . ., K—Kt6; 61 P—R4, P—B7; 62 Kt×P, K×Kt; 63 P—Kt4, and the Black king is too far away. For example, 63 . . ., K—Q6; 64 P—Kt5, K—Q5; 65 K—Kt4, K—K4; 66 K—R5, K—K3; 67 K—Kt6, B—K4; 68 K—R7, K—B2; 69 P—Kt6ch., K—B1; 70 P—R5, B—B3; 71 P—R6, B—K4; 72 P—Kt7ch.

61. P—R4 B—Q3
62. P—Kt4 B—K2
63. P—Kt5 K—K4
64. K—Kt4 B—B1
65. Kt—B2 K—K5

Even at this stage White, who has fought so hard to create a win, has not succeeded. Black draws by 65 . . ., K—K3; 66 P—R5, K—B2; 67 K—B5, K—Kt1; 68 P—R6, K—R2; 69 K—B6, B—Q3; 70 P—Kt 6ch., K×P; 71 P—Kt7, B—K4ch. But even a master, given sufficient opportunities for going wrong, will frequently do so sooner or later.

66. P—R5 K—Q6
67. Kt—R1 K—K5
68. P—R6 K—K4
69. K—R5 K—B4
70. Kt—B2 B—Q3
71. Kt—Q4ch.

An elegant knight manœuvre, allowing the Black Pawn forward one square in order to free his own pawns from the attention of the Black king.

71. K—K5
72. Kt—K2 P—B7
73. P—Kt6 B—R6
74. P—Kt7 K—Q6
75. P—Kt8=Q

Decisively creating the fifth queen to have appeared on the board in this superb game.

75. K×Kt
76. Q—R2 Resigns.

W. E. Napier (b. 1881) was taken from England to America as a child and in 1908 assumed American nationality. He was known as a child prodigy and won the championship of the Brooklyn chess club at the age of fifteen. In 1904 he won the British championship, but in the following year retired absolutely from the game.

GAME 23

LASKER–NAPIER

Cambridge Springs tournament, 1904.

SICILIAN DEFENCE

1.	P—K4	P—QB4
2.	Kt—QB3	Kt—QB3
3.	Kt—B3	P—KKt3
4.	P—Q4	P×P
5.	Kt×P	B—Kt2
6.	B—K3	P—Q3
7.	P—KR3	Kt—B3
8.	P—KKt4	

An advance justified not by the position but by Lasker's own ability. Black's attempt to disprove the move leads to a game of enthralling complexity.

8.		O—O
9.	P—Kt5	Kt—K1
10.	P—KR4	Kt—B2
11.	P—B4	P—K4
12.	Kt(4)—K2	P—Q4

Overestimating his position, though the ensuing course of the game shows that Black had sound reasons for believing that by this move he would secure the advantage. Correct was B—Kt5.

13. KP×P

(BLACK) NAPIER

(WHITE) LASKER

Position before Black's 13th move.

(DIAGRAM 30)

13.		Kt—Q5
14.	Kt×Kt	

If B×Kt, P×B; 15 Kt×P, Kt×P; 16 Q—Q2, R—K1ch.; 17 B—K2, and Black can recover his pawn with the better game by Kt×P.

14.		Kt×P

Beginning to force White's hand. 15 Kt×Kt is no reply now as P×Kt would win by 16 B×P, Q×Kt; 17 B×B, Q×R; 18 B×R, Q×Pch.

15. Kt—B5 Kt×Kt
16. Q×Q

If P×Kt, B×Kt; 17 P×P, B×KP; 18 B—Q4, B—Kt6ch.; 19 B—B2 (K—Q2, Q—Q4; 20 R—KKt1, B—B5ch.), Q—B2; with the better game.

16. R×Q
17. Kt—K7ch.

If Kt×B, Kt—Q4; 18 O—O—O, B—Kt5; and White cannot play 19 R—Q3, for then Kt×B; 20 R×Kt, R—Q8 Mate. Also if 17 P×Kt, B×Kt; 18 P×P, B×P; 19 B—Q2, B—Kt6ch.; with advantage. The shrewdness of Black's calculation on his 12th move is becoming apparent, and White must find the very best move every time to escape defeat. But at the same time White is quietly preparing his own plans against the Black king, as will soon appear.

17. K—R1
18. P—R5

In his increasingly difficult position, White exercises every subtlety to elude disaster. P×Kt, so far from winning a piece, would actually lose by P×P; 19 B—Q4, B×B; 20 P×B, R—K1; while if 18 Kt×B, Kt—Q4; retains for Black his material and positional advantage. The text move suddenly threatens a winning attack by 19 RP×P, BP×P; 20 Kt×Pch., K—Kt1; 21 B—B4ch., Kt—Q4; 22 B×Ktch., R×B; 23 Kt—K7ch.

18. R—K1
19. B—B5 P×RP

It is Black who must now take care not to lose a piece. If P×BP; 20 P×P, P×P; 21 B—B4, threatening both Kt×P Mate and B—B7. While if 19 . . ., Kt—K5; 20 RP×P, BP×P; 21 B—Kt5, B—B4 (not R—Q1; 22 B—B4); 22 B×R, R×B (not Kt×B; 23 B×P); 23 Kt×B, Kt×B; 24 Kt×B. The unlikely text move is the solution to his problem; he will sacrifice the exchange to obtain a probable draw with his two bishops.

20. B—B4

If P×Kt, B—B1; 21 B—Kt5, R×Kt; 22 B×R, B×B; with excellent drawing chances. White, who has throughout accepted all Black's challenges, prefers to continue his threats to the Black king.

20. P×P

The alternative, giving chances of a draw, was B—K3; 21 B×B, P×B; 22 P×Kt, B—B1; 23 R×P, B×Kt; 24 B×B, R×B; 25 P×P, R—QB1; 26 O—O—O, R×P; 27 P—Kt6, but Black has yet another surprise by which he hopes to win.

21.	B×P	Kt—K5
22.	B×R	B×P
23.	R—QKt1	B—B6ch.
24.	K—B1	B—KKt5

(BLACK) NAPIER

(WHITE) LASKER

Position before White's 25th move.

(DIAGRAM 31)

The key move of Black's plan. White is now faced with no less than four threats, R×B, Kt×B, Kt—Q7ch., and Kt—Kt6ch. He can only return his material advantage, for a move like 25 K—Kt2, would simply create another threat in the advance of Black's BP.

25.	KB×P	B×B
26.	R×B	Kt—Kt6ch.
27.	K—Kt2	Kt×R
28.	R×P	

The complications are over, and the material is still level. It will soon be seen, however, that White's position is now superior.

28.		P—R4
29.	R—Kt3	B—Kt2
30.	R—KR3	Kt—Kt6
31.	K—B3	

And now White secures his first material advantage, one pawn. 31 . . ., B—K4; is now answered by Kt—Kt6ch., but more deadly to Black is the threat of P—Kt6.

31.		R—R3
32.	K×P	Kt—K7ch.
33.	K—B5	Kt—B6
34.	P—R3	Kt—R5
35.	B—K3	Resigns.

It is rare indeed that two masters, both with considerable justification, play to outcombine one another in the same combination.

O. Duras (b. 1882) was a brilliant Czech player of the first decade of the twentieth century. He won tournaments against the strongest opposition, notably sharing 1st prize at Prague, 1908, and Vienna, 1908. After 1914 he retired from active play.

R. Teichmann (1868–1925), a German who lived for many years in England, promised at one time to become one of the world's strongest masters, but eye trouble forced him to abandon the practice of the game. His greatest success was winning the tournament at Carlsbad, 1911.

GAME 24

DURAS–TEICHMANN

Ostend tournament, 1906.

Ruy Lopez

1.	P—K4	P—K4
2.	Kt—KB3	Kt—QB3
3.	B—Kt5	P—QR3
4.	B—R4	Kt—B3
5.	O—O	B—K2
6.	R—K1	P—Q3
7.	P—B3	O—O
8	P—KR3	P—R3

Black plays a restricted variation of the defence.

9.	P—Q4	B—Q2
10.	QKt—Q2	R—K1
11.	Kt—B1	B—KB1
12.	Kt—Kt3	P—KKt3
13.	B—Kt3	Q—K2
14.	B—K3	B—Kt2

The purpose of White's last move would appear if Black played Kt—QR4 here, for then 15 P×P, P×P; 16 Kt×P, Kt×B; 17 P×Kt, Q×Kt; 18 B—Q4, Q—K2; 19 B×Kt, Q×B; 20 Q×B, winning a pawn.

15.	P—Q5	Kt—Q1
16.	P—B4	P—Kt3
17.	B—B2	P—QR4
18.	Kt—R2	K—R2
19.	R—Kt1	Kt—Kt1
20.	P—B4	P×P

After a typical Lopez period of preparation Black now has to make up his mind how to deal with White's first aggressiveness. If he does not capture the pawn, he may be faced with either 21 P—B5, or 21 Kt—B3 and 22 P×P. In the latter case he would have to recapture on K4 with the pawn on Q3, and then White's QR suddenly assumes a much more menacing aspect after P—QR3, P—QKt4 and P—QB5.

21.	B×P	B—K4

To permit 22 P—K5 would be to allow the full force of White's attack to develop against his king. By exchanging bishops and getting his queen off the K file the threat is largely diminished.

22. B×B Q×B
23. Kt—K2 Q—Kt2
24. Kt—KB3 Kt—Kt2
25. Kt—Kt3 Kt—B4
26. Q—Q2 R—K2
27. Q—B2 QR—K1

It has been suggested that here 28 P—K5 must be prevented not for positional but for combinative reasons, the continuation given being 28 . . ., P×P; 29 Kt—R5, Q—R1; 30 R×P, R×R; 31 Kt—Kt 5ch., P×Kt; 32 Q×Pch., K—R3; 33 Q×P Mate. However, there seems no valid objection to 29 . . ., Q—B1; 30 R or Kt ×P, QR—K1; beyond the fact that White's position has been improved by the pawn advance.

28. R—K2 K—R1
29. P—Kt3 Kt—B3
30. QR—K1 Kt—R2
31. B—Kt1 Kt—Kt4
32. Kt×Kt

Double-edged. He will now have to prevent Black's P—Kt5 and this lets the queen take up a strong position on the Black squares. In addition it gives Black an open file against the White king.

32. P×Kt
33. Q—B3 Q—Q5ch.
34. K—R2 K—Kt2
35. R—KB2

To give his king a flight square on Kt1 after 35 . . ., P—Kt5; 36 P×P, R—R1ch.

35. Q—K4
36. R(K)—KB1 R—KR1
37. K—Kt1 R—R5
38. Q—K3 R—R3

The position is full of complications. After White's last move P—Kt5 would be answered by 39 Kt—B5ch., B×Kt; 40 R×B, P×R; 41 Q—Kt5ch., K—B1; 42 Q×R, P×KP; 43 R—B6 (threatening Q—R8 Mate), K—K1; 44 Q ×P.

39. P—R3 P—Kt5
40. P×P B×P
41. R—B4 B—Q2
42. Q—B2 B—K1
43. R—B5 Q—B6

Again frustrating White's attempts to develop a combinative win. If instead P×R; 44 Kt×Pch., K—R2; 45 Kt×R(6), K×Kt; 46 Q—R4ch., K—Kt2 (Q—R4; 47 R—B 6ch.); 47 R—B3, Kt×KP; 48 B×Kt, Q×B; 49 R—Kt3ch, and mates. But at last White has succeeded in forcing P—K5 and getting his bishop into the attack.

44. P—K5 P×P
45. R—Kt5 K—R2

[Diagram 32]

46. Kt—B5

Very fine. He forces the pace with a move Black had taken steps to prevent.

46. P×Kt
47. Q×Pch. R—Kt3

Not K—R1; 48 R—R5, Q—K6ch.; 49 K—R2, P—K5 (Kt

(BLACK) TEICHMANN

(WHITE) DURAS

Position before White's 46th move.

(DIAGRAM 32)

—Q2; 50 R—B3, Q—Q7; 51 R×Rch., Q×R; 52 R—R3); 50 Q—B6ch., K—R2 (K—Kt1; 51 R×R); 51 R(1)—B5, R—Q2; 52 R(B)—Kt5, and mates.

48. Q—B6

With the triple threats of Q×R(7), B×Rch. and R—R5 ch. In this precarious position Black starts a vigorous counter-attack.

48. Q—Q5ch.
49. R—B2

If K—R2, Q—R5ch.; 50 K—Kt1, Q×R; winning.

49. Q—Q8ch.
50. K—R2 P—K5

By stopping two of the threats his immediate loss is limited to the exchange, and his counter-attack continues.

51. Q×R R—R3ch.
52. K—Kt3 Q—K8

Much stronger than Q×KtP ch., 53 R—B3. The threat 53..., Q—K6ch.; puts both White rooks in jeopardy.

53. Q×B Q—K6ch.
54. K—Kt4 P—B4ch.

Of course not Q×R; 55 Q—Kt8 Mate. Against the text move White must be careful. If 55 K×P, Q×R(7)ch.; and mates next move, while if 55 R(2)×P, there is perpetual check by Q—K7ch.; 56 K—B4 (K—Kt3, Q—K6ch.), Q—B7ch.; 57 K—K5, Q—Kt7ch.

55. R(5)×P R—Kt3ch.
56. Q×Rch.

The climax of Black's counter-attack. White cannot play K—R4 because of Q—Kt6ch.; 57 K—R5, R—R3 Mate. So he must give up queen for rook. But his two rooks are in co-operation and will still be strong enough to win.

56. K×Q
57. R—B6ch. K—Kt2
58. R—B7ch. K—Kt1
59. R—B8ch. K—Kt2
60. R(2)—B7ch. K—Kt3
61. R—B6ch. K—Kt2
62. R(8)—B7ch. K—Kt1
63. K—R5

Threatening mate in two.

63. Q—K7ch.
64. P—Kt4 Resigns.

If Q—R7ch.; 65 K—Kt6, and there are no more checks. A fine example of attack and defence.

A. Rubinstein (b. 1882), a Pole by birth, came rapidly into prominence early in the 1900's. His style was quiet and simple but always extremely effective and frequent tournament successes, such as his 1st prizes at Carlsbad, 1907, and Pistyan, 1912, and his tie for first place with Lasker at St. Petersburg, 1909, brought him into consideration as a challenger for the world title but he never secured a match. He retired in 1930 suffering with a mental breakdown from which he has never fully recovered.

GAME 25

RUBINSTEIN–LASKER

St. Petersburg tournament, 1909.

TARRASCH DEFENCE

1. P—Q4 P—Q4
2. Kt—KB3 Kt—KB3
3. P—B4 P—K3
4. B—Kt5 P—B4

An inferior move which comes better after 4 Kt—B3, as he can then continue P—B4; 5 B—Kt5, P×QP; 6 KKt×P, P—K4. Now White removes the pawn from the K file and he is left with a weak isolated pawn.

5. BP×P KP×P
6. Kt—B3 P×P
7. KKt×P Kt—B3

Inviting 8 B×Kt, Q×B; 9 Kt×P, Q×Kt; 10 Kt—B 7ch., K—Q1; 11 Kt×R, B—Kt5ch.

8. P—K3 B—K2
9. B—Kt5 B—Q2

He could play to hold the pawn by Q—Q3 but then 10 B—KB4, or by Q—Q2 but then 10 Q—R4, in both cases with a difficult game. He prefers to give up the pawn with the chance of a quick counter-attack.

10. QB×Kt B×B
11. Kt×P B×Kt
12. P×B Q—Kt4

The point. If White continues 13 Kt—B7ch., then 13 . . ., K—Q1; 14 B×Kt, B×B; 15 P—Q5 (Kt×R, R—K1ch.), K×Kt; 16 P×B, QR—Q1; 17 Q—B2, KR—K1ch.; 18 K—B1, Q—Kt4ch.; with at least an equal game.

13. B×Kt B×B
14. Kt—K3 O—O—O

Somewhat better was B×P; 15 R—KKt1, Q—R4ch.; 16 Q—Q2, Q×Qch.; 17 K×Q, B—K5; and if 18 R×P, B—Kt3.

15. O—O KR—K1
16. R—B1

(BLACK) LASKER

(WHITE) RUBINSTEIN

Position before Black's 16th move.

(DIAGRAM 33)

16. R×Kt

Threatening Q×P Mate. Black has brought all his forces into play in the minimum of time, and White will have great difficulty in preventing him from equalising, but since White can do so 16 . . ., K—Kt1 ; was better.

17. R×Bch. P×R
18. Q—B1

Taking counter measures just in time. The complications are considerable even though all the minor pieces are gone. If Black defends his QBP White takes the rook and remains a pawn ahead.

18. R×P

A splendid move. Now after 19 Q×Pch., K—Kt1 ; there are no more checks and White must continue 20 P×R, Q×Pch. ; 21 K—R1, Q—K7 ; 22 R—KKt1 (there are astonishingly enough still no checks), R—Q8 ; and the draw is almost inevitable.

19. P×R

But White has no intention of letting Black get the draw. Now if 19 . . ., R—Q3 ; 20 R×P, with much the better game, so the QBP falls after all.

19. R—Q2
20. Q×Pch. K—Q1

Not R—B2 ; 21 Q—R8ch., K—Q2 ; 22 R×Pch., K—K3 ; 23 Q—K8ch. (R×R, Q×Pch. ; 24 K—B1, Q—Q6ch. ; 25 K—B2, Q—Q7ch. ; 26 K—B3, Q—Q6ch. ; 27 K—Kt4, Q—B4ch. ; 28 K—R4, Q—B5ch. ; recovering the rook with a probable draw), K—Q3 ; 24 R×R, winning.

21. R—B4 P—B4

Both players fight all the way. Now if R—Q8ch. ; 22 K—B2, R—Q7ch. ; 23 K—K1, Q×P ; 24 R—Q4ch., K—K2 ; 25 Q—Q6ch., wins.

22. Q—B5

At last White establishes his advantage. Black cannot defend the BP by P—Kt3 because of 23 Q—B8ch., K—B2 ; 24 R—B4ch., K—Kt3 ; 25 Q—Kt4ch., K—R3 ; 26 R—B6 Mate.

22. Q—K2
23. Q×Qch.

Removing the piece that is most likely to give Black drawing chances in spite of a material inferiority.

23.		K×Q
24.	R×P	R—Q8ch.
25.	K—B2	R—Q7ch.
26.	K—B3	R×QKtP
27.	R—QR5	

He has come through a harassing time into a won rook ending. There are, however, so many positions in rook endings where the extra pawn does not win that he still has to be very careful how he forces the position.

27.		R—Kt2
28.	R—R6	K—B1
29.	P—K4	R—B2
30.	P—KR4	K—B2
31.	P—Kt4	K—B1
32.	K—B4	K—K2
33.	P—R5	P—R3
34.	K—B5	K—B2
35.	P—K5	R—Kt2
36.	R—Q6	K—B1
37.	R—R6	

If K—Kt6, K—K1; 38 P—K6, R—Kt5; 39 K×P, R×Pch.; 40 K×P, and there are still technical difficulties in White's way.

37.		K—B2
38.	R—Q6	K—B1
39.	R—B6	

If R—Q8ch., K—K2; 40 R—KKt8, K—B2; and if 39 K—Kt6, R—Kt5; 40 R—Q8ch., K—K2; 41 R—KKt8, R×Pch.

39.		K—B2
40.	P—R3	

A delightful conclusion, preventing R—Kt5. Now after 40 . . ., K—B1; 41 K—Kt6, R—Q2; 42 R—B8ch., K—K2; 43 R—KKt8, R—Q5(K—K3; 44 R—K8ch., K—Q4; 45 P—K6); 44 R×Pch., K—K3; 45 K×P, with two united passed pawns. Therefore—

Resigns.

J. R. Capablanca (1888–1942), a Cuban, began playing as a child, was champion of Cuba at the age of 12, of America at 21 and of the world at 33. His style was simple and almost mechanical, of an accuracy which reduced opponents to despair; he won a series of tournament victories from 1910 to 1936, and it was only after he lost the world title in 1927 that his infallibility was called into question.

GAME 26

MARSHALL–CAPABLANCA

11th match game,
New York, 1909.

PILLSBURY ATTACK

1. P—Q4 P—Q4
2. P—QB4 P—K3
3. Kt—QB3 Kt—KB3
4. B—Kt5 B—K2
5. P—K3 Kt—K5
6. B×B Q×B
7. B—Q3

This allows Black to open the long diagonal for his bishop. The more normal line is Kt—B3, Kt—Q2; 8 Q—B2, followed either by Kt×Kt; 9 P×Kt, or by P—QB3; 9 Kt×Kt, P×Kt; 10 Q×P, Q—Kt 5ch.

7. Kt×Kt
8. P×Kt P×P
9. B×BP P—QKt3
10. Q—B3

He cannot hold the diagonal, but this move leads to more combinative possibilities than the usual Kt—B3.

10. P—QB3
11. Kt—K2 B—Kt2
12. O—O O—O
13. P—QR4

To prevent P—QKt4; 14B—Q3, P—QB4; 15 Q—Kt3, P—B5; 16 B—B2, P—QR4.

13. P—QB4
14. Q—Kt3 Kt—B3
15. Kt—B4 QR—B1
16. B—R2

If B—Kt3, Kt—R4. Black already has the better position.

16. KR—Q1
17. KR—K1 Kt—R4
18. QR—Q1

Sacrificing the RP to obtain open lines in the centre by P—K4 or P—Q5.

18. B—B3
19. Q—Kt4 P—B5

If at once B×RP; 20 Kt×P, P×Kt; 21 B×Pch., K—R1; 22 B×R, B×R; 23 R×B, and it is White who is a pawn ahead.

20. P—Q5

P—K4 first gives a more enduring pressure.

20. B×RP

If P×P; 21 Kt×P, B×Kt; 22 R×B, R×R; 23 Q×Rch., R—Q1; and Black has no advantage.

21. R—Q2 P—K4

He must either submit to an attack on his king, or by playing P×P allow White freedom in the centre.

22. Kt—R5 P—Kt3

He cannot avoid this weakening move, for if Q—B1; 23, B—Kt1, and P—Kt3 must follow, for 23 . . ., R—Q3 (preventing Kt—B6ch.) is answered by 24 Kt×P.

23. P—Q6

(BLACK) CAPABLANCA

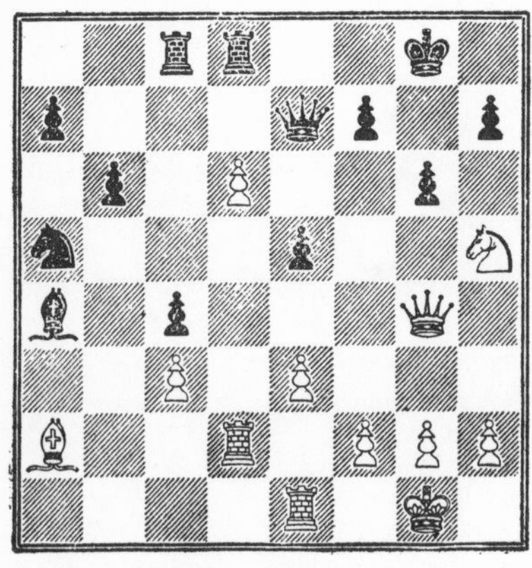

(WHITE) MARSHALL

Position before Black's 23rd move.

(DIAGRAM 34)

23. Q—K3
24. Q—Kt5 K—R1

If R×P at once, 25 R×R, Q×R; 26 Q—R6, Q—B1; 27 Kt—B6ch., and mates.

25. Kt—B6 R×P
26. R×R Q×R
27. B—Kt1

Q—R4 would be answered by K—Kt2.

27. Kt—B3
28. B—B5 R—Q1

P×B would permit 29 Q—R6.

29. P—R4

B—Q7 would prevent Black's next move, but White is two pawns down and therefore in haste to increase his pressure.

29. Kt—K2
30. Kt—K4 Q—B2
31. Q—B6ch. K—Kt1
32. B—K6 P×B

White continues to attack with ingenuity, and the defence has to be a model of fighting carefulness. If R—KB1; 33 Kt—Kt5, P×B; 34 Q×Rch., K×Q; 35 Kt×Pch, winning the exchange.

33. Q×KPch. K—B1
34. Kt—Kt5 Kt—Kt1
35. P—B4 R—K1
36. P×P

[Diagram 35]

The attack seems to have been beaten off, but White evolves still more surprises. Black still loses the exchange if he takes the queen.

36. R—K2
37. R—B1ch. K—Kt2

(BLACK) CAPABLANCA

(WHITE) MARSHALL

Position before Black's 36th move.

(DIAGRAM 35)

38. P—R5 B—K1
39. P—R6ch. K—R1

Not K × P ; 40 Q—Kt4, K—Kt2 ; 41 Kt—K6ch., nor Kt × P ; 40 Q—B6ch.

40. Q—Q6 Q—B4

The attack continues. If now Q×Q ; 41 P×Q, R—Q2 ; 42 R—B8, R×P ; 43 R×B, and the threat of Kt—B7ch., wins. If 41 . . ., R—K4 ; 42 P—Q7, B×P ; 43 Kt—B7 Mate. And if 41 . . ., R×P ; 42 R—B7, B×R ; 43 Kt×B Mate.

41. Q—Q4

Black is threatening Q×Pch., and if 41 Q×Q, P×Q ; 42 R—B8, R×P ; 43 R×B, R×Kt ; and Black wins.

41. R×P

P—K6 dis. ch., must be stopped, but if Q×P ; 42 R—B8 (not Q×Qch., R×Q ; 43 R—B7, R—K2), Q×Q (forced by the threat of R×B) ; 43 KP×Q, B—B3 ; 44 Kt—B7ch., R×Kt ; 45 R×R, Kt×P ; 46 R×P, with good drawing chances.

42. Q—Q7 R—K2

The defence holds out against White's last brilliant fling. Fatal would be B×Q ; 43 Kt—B7 Mate. Had White tried 42 R—B7, the text move would have equally sufficed, but then 42 . . ., Kt×P ; would have been stronger.

43. R—B7 B×Q

Or R×Q ; 44 R×R, Kt×P ; but not 44 . . ., B×R ; 45 Kt—B7 Mate. A perfect demonstration of the power even of an unsound attack and of the inexorable justice that must come if the defence is correct.

Resigns.

C. Schlechter (1873–1918), of Vienna, early earned the unenviable title of "drawing master," though at his best he was as fine a stylist as any player of his time. However, when he shared 1st prize both at Vienna, 1908, and Prague, 1908, he was recognised for the great player he was. In 1910 he played and drew a match for the world title and oddly enough he only failed to win by not playing for a draw. He died of under-nourishment in 1918.

GAME 27

SCHLECHTER–LASKER

7th match game, Berlin, 1910.

Sicilian Defence

1. P—K4 P—QB4
2. Kt—KB3 Kt—QB3
3. P—Q4 P×P
4. Kt×P Kt—B3
5. Kt—QB3 P—KKt3
6. B—QB4 P—Q3
7. Kt×Kt

Introducing the sharp Magnus Smith variation.

7. P×Kt
8. P—K5 Kt—Kt5
9. P—K6

Magnus Smith's own analysis continued 9 B—B4, P—Q4; 10 Kt×P, P×Kt; 11 B×P, B—K3; 12 B—B6ch., B—Q2; 13 B×R, Q×B; 14 O—O, but a later improvement is 9 . . ., Q—Kt3; 10 Q—B3, B—B4; 11 P×P, P×P; 12 O—O, O—O—O; 13 KR—K1, P—Q4; 14 P—KR3. Black is just able to evolve a satisfactory defence against the text.

9. P—KB4
10. O—O B—KKt2

If P—Q4; 11 Kt×P.

11. B—B4 Q—Kt3
12. B—QKt3

There is nothing in 12 Q—B3, B—Kt2.

12. B—QR3
13. Kt—R4 Q—Q5
14. Q×Q

The immediate exchange of queens is virtually forced, for if 14 Q—B3, then Q—K5; 15 Q×Q, P×Q; 16 P—B4, O—O; and Black gains a move on the variation actually played.

14. B×Q
15. P—B4 O—O
16. QR—Q1 B—B3

An inaccuracy, allowing White to develop ingenious winning chances by sacrificing his QB. Better was either Kt—K4 or B—K4 blocking the bishop.

17. KR—K1 P—Kt4
18. B×QP P×B
19. R×P

(BLACK) LASKER

(WHITE) SCHLECHTER

Position before Black's 19th move.

(DIAGRAM 36)

Now White has a powerful attacking position with the threats of P—B5 followed by P—K7 dis. ch., and of P—KR3 and P—K7 followed by R×B. Only the most determined and accurate resistance by Black can hold the game. He has to let his QBP go in order to hold up the dangerous KP and whether he tries 19 . . ., B—K4; or 19 . . ., B—K2; the reply is still 20 P—B5.

19. B—K4
20. P—B5 KR—K1

Not 20 . . ., B×R; 21 P—K7 dis. ch., K—Kt2; 22 P×B, KR—K1; 23 P—Q7, winning.

21. P—Kt3

Now the subtlety of Black's defence in choosing 19 . . ., B—K4; is clear. If 21 P—KR3, B—R7ch.; 22 K—R1, B×R; 23 P×B, Kt×Pch.; 24 K—Kt1, Kt—K5; 25 P—K7 dis. ch., K—Kt2; and the pawns are held.

21. B—B3

Still not B×R; 22 P—K7 dis. ch., K—Kt2; 23 P×B, Kt—B3; 24 Kt—B5 (the move not available to White in the previous note), B—B1; 25 B—R4.

22. R×P B—QKt2

Insufficient would be B—Kt 4; 23 R—Q6, B—K4 (B×Kt; 24 B×B, R—K2; 25 B—Q7); 24 P—KR3, B×R; 25 P×B, Kt—B3; 26 Kt—B5.

23. R—B7 B—K5
24. Kt—B3 B×Kt

If B—Q5; 25 Kt×B, P×Kt; 26 R×KP, B×Pch.; 27 K—Kt2, Kt—B3; 28 R—QKt4, B—K6; 29 R(4)—Kt7, and Black is in zugswang.

25. P×B Kt—K4

Black's defence has been so far successful that the worst threats are over though the passed pawns remain. He is now able to interpolate a little attack of his own.

26. R—Q1 Kt—B6ch.
27. K—B1 Kt×Pch.
28. K—K1

Of course not 28 K—K2, B—B6ch.

28. Kt—B6ch.
29. K—K2 Kt—K4
30. R(1)—Q7

Recovering the pawn, for if 30 . . ., P—KR3; 31 R—Kt 7ch., K—B1; 32 R—R7, threatening mate. Black's defence still has to be extremely accurate.

30. P—B5
31. R—Kt7ch. K—R1
32. R×KtP B—Q6ch.

Now Black suddenly produces a threat to win the game himself. Of course White cannot reply 33 K—Q2 because of Kt—B6ch.

33. K—Q1 P×P

The point. White cannot play 34 R×Kt because of P×P; 35 R—B7, R—KB1; winning.

34. P×P Kt—Kt3
35. R—Q5 B—K5
36. R—Q6 B—B4
37. B—Q5 QR—Kt1
38. P—B6 Kt—B1
39. R—QKt7

Temporarily holding the KP, for if now 39 . . ., Kt×P; 40 R×R, with a winning rook ending.

39. QR—B1
40. P—K7 Kt—Kt3
41. B—B7 R×KP
42. B×Kt B—Kt5ch.

Although he has two pieces *en prise* Black can save both of them owing to the position of White's king, and in fact this enables him to save the game. He now succeeds in remaining a piece ahead.

43. K—B1 R—K8ch.
44. K—Kt2 P×B
45. R×KtP B—B4
46. R—B6 B—K5
47. R×P R—Kt8ch.
48. K—R3 B×P

Drawn.

The culmination of a magnificently accurate defence. Both of White's advanced passed pawns have fallen and Black now threatens B—Kt4 followed by R×P Mate. White has nothing better than to take perpetual check.

Jacques Mieses (b. 1865) played in his first masters tournament at Hastings, 1895, and what may be his last at Hastings, 1946. His style was extremely aggressive and he delighted in such risky gambits as the Danish. This brought him uneven results in tournaments, little success in matches, but frequent brilliancy prizes.

GAME 28

MIESES–CAPABLANCA

Exhibition game, Berlin, 1913.

Centre Game

1.	P—K4	P—K4
2.	P—Q4	P×P
3.	Q×P	Kt—QB3
4.	Q—K3	Kt—B3
5.	Kt—QB3	B—Kt5
6.	B—Q2	O—O
7.	O—O—O	R—K1

By simple play against White's risky opening Black has secured the win of a pawn. If now 8 P—B3, P—Q4; and then if 9 B—Q3, P—Q5.

8.	Q—Kt3	Kt×P
9.	Kt×Kt	R×Kt
10.	B—KB4	Q—B3

Not liking P—Q3 which would allow White a strong attack for the pawn. If now 11 B×P, Q—K3; 12 K—Kt1, R—K8; 13 B—K2, R×Rch.; 14 B×R, Q—K8; 15 Q—B3, P—Q3; with the threat of Q—K2.

11.	Kt—R3	P—Q3
12.	B—Q3	Kt—Q5

R—K1 would lead to variations similar to those in the previous note. He did not like them then, and similarly prefers now to indulge in complications based upon the threat of Kt—K7ch., which would allow simplification without retreat.

13. B—K3

Naturally not B×R, Kt—K7ch.; winning the queen. Also, if P—QB3, Kt—K7ch.; 14 B×Kt, R×B; and White cannot play 15 P×B because of Q×P Mate.

13. B—Kt5

Overcomplicated. Correct was R—Kt5; 14 B×Kt, R×B; 15 P—QB3, B×P; 16 P×B, R—KKt5; 17 Q—K3, Q×Pch.

[Diagram 37]

14. Kt—Kt5

White must exercise the utmost care. 14 QR—Kt1, Kt—K7ch.; 15 B×Kt, B×B; is far too unenterprising. 14 P—KB3 only gives equality after R×B; 15 Q×B. If 14 P—QB 3, then B×P is a possible reply, for if 15 P×B, Kt—K7ch.; 16

(BLACK) CAPABLANCA

(WHITE) MIESES

Position before White's 14th move.

(DIAGRAM 37)

B×Kt, Q×Pch.; (the White queen was defending this on the previous move); 17 K—Kt1, R—Kt5 Mate. And finally if 14 B×Kt, R×B; 15 P—QB3, B×R; 16 R×B, R×B; 17 Q×R, B—B4; with a pawn ahead. Black's combination is seen in all its ingenuity.

14. R×B

The only move. If White now takes the rook, Black plays B×R and still comes out a pawn ahead.

15. Q×B Kt—K7ch.

By his last move White has proved the whole combination to have been unsound after all. Black must now lose the exchange, for if R—K2; 16 B×Pch., K—B1; 17 R×Kt, wins a piece.

16. B×Kt R×B
17. Kt—K4

A tactical finesse, enabling him to capture on K4 instead of on K2. With the exchange ahead in this simplified position, any player might expect to win.

17. R×Kt
18. Q×R Q—Kt4ch.

The alternative of B—B4; 19 Q×P, Q—Q1; was not enticing.

19. P—B4 Q—Kt4
20. P—B3 B—B4
21. KR—K1 Q—B3
22. R—Q5

An error of judgment. He cannot force the K side and get a quick mate by weight of material, so the logical course was 22 Q×Q, P×Q; 23 R—K7, with a winning end-game.

22. Q—Q2
23. P—B5

And here Q—K7 with the same idea was better. Black could not reply Q—Kt5 because of 24 Q—K8ch. Now that White has wasted two moves, Black, whose position still does not appear to hold any promise, brings all his pieces to bear on White's king with an economy of moves that is quite remarkable.

23. P—QB3
24. R—Q2 P—Q4
25. Q—B3 B—K2

Preventing P—B6 and threatening B—Kt4.

26. R(2)—K2 B—B3
27. Q—R5 P—KR3
28. P—KKt4 K—R2
29. K—Kt1 R—Q1

The first stage. P—Q5 is threatened.

30. R—Q1 P—B4
31. Q—R3 Q—R5
32. R(2)—Q2 Q—K5ch.
33. K—R1 P—QKt4

And now the threat of P—Kt5 is worse still. The way in which Black has seized the initiative is an object lesson in the correct use of material.

34. Q—Kt2 Q—R5
35. K—Kt1

Not R×P, B—Q5; or even Q×Rch.

35. P—Kt5
36. P×P Q×P
37. P—QR3

If now R×P, R—QKt1; 38 R(5)—Q2, P—B5; with variations similar to those in the actual game.

37. Q—R5
38. R×P R—QKt1
39. R(5)—Q2
[Diagram 38]

39. P—B5

Much stronger than Q×RP.

40. Q—Kt3 R—Kt6

Not P—B6; 41 Q×R, P×R; 42 R×P. The text move, followed by P—B6, makes defence of the RP an urgent necessity.

(BLACK) CAPABLANCA

(WHITE) MIESES

Position before Black's 39th move.

(DIAGRAM 38)

41. Q—Q6 P—B6
42. R—QB2 P×P
43. R—Q3 Q—K5

White has battled hard to stave off the attack and just when he seems to have succeeded Black prevents R×R by the double threat of Q—K8ch. and R×R.

44. R—Q1 R—QB6

And with this beautiful conclusion Black settles the matter. He has not only escaped defeat but has actually won a lost game.

Resigns

For if 45 R—Q2, R×R; 46 R×R, Q—K8ch.; and if 45 Q—Q2, R×P; the very move White has fought so long to prevent.

GAME 29

CAPABLANCA–MARSHALL

New York tournament, 1918.

RUY LOPEZ

1.	P—K4	P—K4
2.	Kt—KB3	Kt—QB3
3.	B—Kt5	P—QR3
4.	B—R4	Kt—B3
5.	O—O	B—K2
6.	R—K1	P—QKt4
7.	B—Kt3	O—O
8.	P—B3	P—Q4

The Marshall Variation, in which a pawn is sacrificed for a strong attack, was introduced to master play in this game.

9.	P×P	Kt×P
10.	Kt×P	Kt×Kt
11.	R×Kt	Kt—B3
12.	R—K1	

Subsequently 12 P—Q4, B—Q3; 13 R—K2, was preferred as a defence, but Capablanca is out of the book and has to improvise. He said afterwards that as soon as Marshall allowed him to play the Ruy Lopez, he suspected a prepared variation was coming, for Marshall had never faced a Ruy Lopez from Capablanca since his unhappy experience against it in the match of 1909. Capablanca anticipated that the attack would be "terrific."

12.		B—Q3
13.	P—KR3	

P—Q4, Kt—Kt5; 14 P—KR3, Q—R5; 15 Q—B3, would merely be a transposition of moves.

13.		Kt—Kt5

The attack begins and with it a period of intense crisis. If in reply to the text move White plays 14 P×Kt, then Q—R5; 15 P—Kt3, KB×P; 16 P×B, Q×Pch.; 17 K—B1, B×P; 18 Q—B2 (R—K2, B—R6ch.; 19 R—Kt2, Q×Rch.; 20 K—K1, QR—K1ch.), B—R6ch.; 19 K—K2, QR—K1ch.; 20 K—Q1, B—Kt5ch.; winning. Or 15 Q—B3, Q—R7ch.; 16 K—B1, B×P; 17 Q×B, Q—R8 ch.; 18 K—K2, QR—K1ch.

14.	Q—B3	Q—R5
15.	P—Q4	

(BLACK) MARSHALL

(WHITE) CAPABLANCA

Position before Black's 15th move.

(DIAGRAM 39)

15.		Kt×P
16.	R—K2	

If 16 Q×Kt, B—R7ch., (B—Kt6 would allow the brilliant reply 17 Q×Pch., R×Q; 18 R—K8 Mate, showing how delicately the game is now balanced); 17 K—B1, B—Kt 6; 18 Q—K2 (now if Q×Pch. the queen is captured with a check), B×P; 19 P×B, QR—K1; 20 Q×R, Q×Pch.; winning. After the text the attack must ease a little as Black loses a piece.

16. B—KKt5

The attack is continued with the utmost ferocity. If instead 16 . . ., Kt×Pch.; 17 P×Kt, B×P; 18 R—K4, or 16 . . ., B×P; 17 P×B, Kt×Pch.; 18 K—B1, Kt—Kt4; 19 Q—Kt2, but 16 . . ., Kt—Kt5; 17 B—KB4, B—Kt2; 18 P—Q5, Kt—B3; was a playable alternative.

17. P×B B—R7ch.
18. K—B1 B—Kt6
19. R×Kt

White has fought his way into slightly calmer water. He obtains two pieces for the rook, but is still behindhand in development.

19. Q—R8ch.
20. K—K2 B×R
21. B—Q2 B—R5
22. Q—R3 QR—K1ch.
23. K—Q3 Q—B8ch.
24. K—B2 B—B7
25. Q—B3 Q—Kt8
26. B—Q5 P—QB4

A last attempt to revivify his flagging attack, but White is now poised for his counter-thrust. The problem of Q side development is to be solved by the advance of the Q side pawns.

27. P×P B×P
28. P—Kt4 B—Q3
29. P—R4 P—QR4
30. P×KtP P×P
31. R—R6 P×P
32. Kt×P B—Kt5
33. P—Kt6

The picture has now changed completely, and Black is helpless against the passed pawn, for the moment his rook leaves the first rank, White has Q×Pch., available again.

33. B×Kt
34. B×B P—R3
35. P—Kt7 R—K6
36. B×Pch.

Forcing the pawn home, for if in reply 36 . . ., K—R1; 37 R—R8, R×Q; 38 R×Rch., K—R2; 39 R—R8ch., K×R; 40 P—Kt8=Qch., or 36 . . ., K—R2; 37 Q—B5ch., K—R1; 38 B×Pch., K×B; 39 Q—Kt6ch., K—R1; 40 Q×P Mate.

36. R×B
37. P—Kt8=Qch. K—R2
38. R×Pch. Resigns.

It is mate in two after 38 . . ., K×R (P×R; 39 Q×R Mate); 39 Q—R8ch., K—Kt3 or 4; 40 Q—R5 Mate.

A. Alekhine (1892–1946), Russian by birth and French by adoption, was world champion from 1927 to 1946, except for the period 1935–7. At his best he was perhaps the most completely equipped and gifted chessplayer of all time, at home in open and close positions, orthodox and experimental, sound in theory and fiery in imagination. In his early years overshadowed by Lasker and Capablanca he showed by his decisive victories in such tournaments as San Remo, 1930 and Bled, 1931, that in the fullness of maturity he was as great if not greater than they.

GAME 30

RUBINSTEIN–ALEKHINE

London tournament, 1922.

SLAV DEFENCE

1. Kt—KB3 P—Q4
2. P—Q4 Kt—KB3
3. P—B4 P—B3
4. Kt—B3 P×P
5. P—QR4 B—B4
6. P—K3 P—K3
7. B×P B—QKt5
8. O—O O—O
9. Kt—K2

The theme of this opening is control of White's K4, and with the text move Rubinstein evolves an elaborate plan to get rid of Black's QB. The more usual play is Q—K2. From this point the battle for control of the vital square is fought out with all the intensity and persistence of which the players are capable.

9. QKt—Q2
10. Kt—Kt3 B—Kt3
11. Kt—R4 P—B4
12. Kt×B RP×Kt
13. P×P Kt×P
14. Q—K2 KKt—K5
15. Kt×Kt Kt×Kt
16. Q—Kt4 Kt—B3
17. Q—B3 Q—B2
18. P—QKt3 Q—K4
19. R—R2 Kt—K5
20. P—R5

Continuing the attack on his K4 by threatening R—R4 at a suitable moment.

20. KR—Q1
21. B—Kt2 B—B6

Not 21 . . ., Q—KB4; 22 R—R4, B—Q7; 23 B×KP.

22. B×B Kt×B
23. R—B2 P—QKt4

The threat is 24 KR—B1, Kt—Q4; 25 P—K4, and White controls the key squares and comes out with the better game.

24. P×P e.p. P×P
25. KR—B1

Maroczy recommended Q—B4 here.

25. Kt—R7
26. R—K1 P—QKt4
27. B—B1 Kt—B6
28. Q—B4

If 28 P—K4, P—Kt5; and the first stage of the game ends in equality. White prefers a line which will allow him to use the open files in the centre later.

28. Q×Q
29. P×Q P—Kt5
30. P—Kt3 R—R6
31. B—B4 K—B1
32. K—Kt2 K—K2
33. R—K5 R—QB1
34. R—Q2 R—Q1
35. R—B2 R—QB1
36. P—R4 Kt—Q4
37. R(2)—K2

Now White has succeeded in developing a strong game in the centre. The immediate threat is 38 R×Kt and if 37 . . ., Kt—Kt3; 38 B×P, P×B; 39 R×Pch., K—B2; 40 R×Kt, R×P; 41 R—Kt7ch., K—B3; 42 R(2)—K7, with advantage.

37. Kt—B6
38. R—Q2 R—B3
39. P—R5

Trying to increase his pressure by sacrificing a pawn, the object of which is primarily to weaken Black's KP. A new intensity comes into the game.

39. P—B3
40. R—K3 P×P
41. P—B5 P—K4
42. R(3)—Q3

(BLACK) ALEKHINE

(WHITE) RUBINSTEIN

Position before Black's 42nd move.

(DIAGRAM 40)

Threatening R—Q8 followed by R(2)—Q7 Mate.

42. R—R2
43. R—Q8 Kt—K5
44. R(2)—Q5 R—Q3

Not Kt—Q3; 45 R—KKt8, Kt×P; 46 R(5)—Q8, Kt—Q3; 47 R—Kt8.

45. R—KKt8 R—R7

White's attack has reached its full force. He is certain to recover his pawn and he is threatening even worse things. Black swings to counter-attack just in time.

46. R×KtPch. K—B1
47. R—Kt8ch.

Still neither player can tip the scales in his own favour. White must now adopt this very ingenious method either to force a draw or to get back to intercept the attack.

47. K×R
48. R—Q2 dis.ch. K—Kt2
49. R×R(2) R—Q7
50. R×R Kt×R
51. B—Q5

A drawn ending has been reached after all.

51. P—K5
52. P—B4

But this is a serious error, for not only does it give Black a passed pawn but it enables him to keep the White king out of action in a corner. Much better was the line suggested by Burn : 52 P—Kt4, P—R5 (K—R3; 53 K—Kt3, K—Kt4; 54 P—B 4ch., P×P e.p. ; 55 P×P, K×BP ; 56 B—B7) ; 53 K—R3, Kt—B6 ; 54 P—Kt5 (B×P, Kt—Kt4ch.), P×P ; 55 B×P, Kt—Q7 ; 56 B—B2, K—B3 ; 57 K—Kt4, Kt—B8 ; 58 B—Q1, drawing.

52. P—K6
53. K—Kt1 K—B1
54. K—Kt2 K—K2
55. B—Kt8 K—Q3
56. B—B7 K—B4
57. B×P Kt×P

Allowing White to bring his king across at last, but now the Black king is also in range.

58. K—B3 K—Q5
59. B—B7

A last effort to retain some chances by 59 . . ., Kt—Q7ch. ; 60 K—K2, P—Kt6 ; 61 B×P, Kt×B ; 62 P—Kt4, and Black must now be careful for if 62 . . ., Kt—B4 ; 63 P—Kt5, Kt—Q2 ; 64 P—Kt6, wins. Correct is 62 . . ., K—K5 ; 63 P—Kt5, Kt—Q5ch. (K×P(4) ; 62 K×P, draws) ; 64 K—K1, K×P(4) ; winning. The reply chosen by Black crushes any chances remaining for White.

59. K—Q6
60. B×Kt K—Q7
61. B—B4 P—Kt6
62. B×P P—K7

Resigns.

R. Reti (1889–1929), a Czech, was one of the most original masters of the twentieth century and a leader of the school which revolted against the dogmas of Tarrasch and was dubbed "Hypermodern." The chief feature of their theory was that occupation of a square or squares was often less effective and certainly less flexible than remote control. The excesses of the Hypermoderns soon faded but their teachings left their mark and brought new vitality into a chess that was becoming too orthodox. A. Becker was a prominent Austrian master who frequently figured in the prize list of continental tournaments.

GAME 31

RETI–BECKER

Vienna tournament, 1923.

RETI SYSTEM

1. Kt—KB3 Kt—KB3
2. P—B4 P—B4
3. P—KKt3 P—KKt3

White's first three moves constitute the Reti System which was introduced to master play at this time. Black's symmetrical defence causes White no trouble but the more aggressive replies based on 1 . . ., P—Q4; which call for a high degree of positional exactness on White's part, had not yet been developed.

4. B—Kt2 B—Kt2
5. Kt—B3 Kt—B3
6. P—Q3 O—O
7. B—K3 P—Q3
8. P—KR3

Not yet Q—Q2 threatening B—R6, because of 8 . . ., Kt—KKt5.

8. B—Q2
9. Q—Q2 R—Kt1
10. B—R6 Kt—K1
11. P—KR4

Indicating his intention of forsaking the positional basis of the opening and of going in for a combinative attack. The KRP is to be given up to open the file for the rook, but the whole idea is somewhat speculative and out of key.

11. B—Kt5
12. P—R5 P×P

If B×P, White can play 13 Kt—R2, Q—Q2 (preventing P—KKt4); 14 P—B3, P—KKt4; 15 Q×P, B—Kt3; 16 Kt—Kt4, with a strong game.

13. Kt—KR4 Q—Q2
14. B—K4 Kt—Q5

Threatening to break up White's attack completely by 15 . . ., Kt—B7ch.; 16 Q×Kt, B×B.

15. O—O—O P—Kt4
16. P—B3 P—Kt5
17. Kt—Kt5

(BLACK) BECKER

(WHITE) RETI

Position before Black's 17th move.

(DIAGRAM 41)

Black has now developed his own attack and White is in difficulties. If 17 P×B, P×Kt; 18 P×BP, Q—R5 (threatening Q—R6ch.); 19 QR—B1, B×B; 20 Q×B, Q—B7 Mate. Or if 17 **Kt—Q5**, Kt×Pch.; 18 K—Kt1 (K—B2, Q—R5ch.; or Q×Kt, B×Bch.), Kt—B6ch.; 19 Kt×Kt, P×Kt; 20 Q—Kt5, R×Pch.; followed by Q—R5. The QKt file must therefore be kept closed.

17. Kt×Pch.

A fine move, for if in reply 18 Q×Kt, B×Bch.; and Black is two pawns ahead with a comfortable game, while if 18 K—Kt1, Kt—B6ch.; 19 P×Kt, P×P; and wins. White must therefore allow Black to sacrifice his knight for the complete disruption of the White pawns.

18. K—B2 Kt×P
19. P×B Kt×B
20. P×Kt Q—K3
21. Kt—B5

A terrible position for White, faced as he is with a threat to his bishop, threats to three pawns, in two cases with check, and after the fall of the QBP with a threat to the knight. He has to stake everything on his attack on Black's king.

21. Q×BPch.
22. K—Kt1 Q×KPch.
23. K—R1 P×P

Black has secured the remarkable and very unusual bargain of six pawns for a minor piece. Less good would be 23 . . ., Q×P; inviting a direct attack on his king by 24 Kt×B, Kt×Kt; 25 QR—K Kt1, nor is R×Kt satisfactory because of 24 Q—Kt5, Q—K4; 25 B×B, Kt×B; 26 QR—K1, Q—B3; 27 Kt×Pch., winning.

24. B×B Kt×B

After 24 . . ., Q×Kt; 25 B×R, R×Kt; 26 B×P, White with a rook for five somewhat loose pawns is better off.

25. Kt×Kt K×Kt
26. Q—R6ch. K—Kt1

An error under time pressure. After K—R1 White would have great difficulty in saving the game, for if 27 QR—KKt1,

R—Kt1; 28 Kt×QP, P×Kt; 29 Q—B6ch., R—Kt2; 30 Q×QP, R—QB1. As it is White is able to threaten R×Pch., with deadly effect.

27. QR—KKt1 K—R1
28. R×P

The first pawn Black loses is fatal to him. As curious and remarkable a game as any ever played.

28. Q×Rch.
29. Q×Q R—Kt1
30. R×Rch. Resigns.

The continuation might be 30 . . ., K×R; 31 Kt—B7, R—QB1; 32 Kt—Q5, R—K1; 33 Q—R4, K—B1; 34 Q×RP, or 30 . . ., R×R; 31 K—Kt1, P—QR3; 32 Kt—B7, P—QR4; 33 Kt—Q5, P—K3; 34 Kt—B6, R—Kt2; 35 Q—R8 ch. Superior weight must tell.

E. Znosko-Borovsky (b. 1884), a prominent Russian master in the years before the First World War, is best known for his lively and excellent treatises on various phases of the game and is perhaps the greatest teacher of elementary chess of all time.

GAME 32

ZNOSKO-BOROVSKY–ALEKHINE

Paris tournament, 1925.

ALEKHINE DEFENCE

1. P—K4 Kt—KB3
2. P—K5 Kt—Q4
3. P—QB4 Kt—Kt3
4. P—Q4 P—Q3
5. P—B4 P×P
6. BP×P Kt—B3
7. B—K3 B—B4
8. Kt—KB3 P—K3
9. Kt—B3 Kt—Kt5
10. R—B1 P—B4

As Tartakower has said of White's formidable looking pawn advances in this opening, White has his initiative to defend, and with this move Black begins undermining White's centre.

11. P—QR3 P×P
12. B—Kt5

No doubt hoping for 12 . . ., B—K2; 13 B×B, Q×B; 14 Kt—QKt5, Kt—B3; 15 Kt—Q6ch., with a good game, though after 12 . . ., Q—Q2; he can achieve little, and the simple 12 Kt×P was sounder.

12. P×Kt

A startling reply indicating that he is going all out to win.

13. B×Q R×B

The alternative line was P×P; 14 B×Kt, P×R=Q; 15 Q×Q, Kt—B7ch.; 16 K—B2, P×B; and Black, as in the text, has a rook and a minor piece for the queen, but chances of a more rapid development than in the line selected. He prefers to retain a more complicated position at some cost in development.

14. Q—Kt3 P×P
15. Q×P Kt—R5
16. Q—R1

He cannot satisfactorily continue protecting his QB2, but possibly a better line was 16 Q—Kt3, Kt—B4; 17 Q—K3, Kt(5)—K6ch.; 18 B×Kt, Kt×Bch.; 19 K—K2, B—B4; 20 Q—Kt5, Kt×Rch.; but not 16 Q—KB2, B—B4; 17 Q—Kt3, Kt—B7ch.; 18 R×Kt, B×R; threatening R—Q8ch.; 20 K—K2, Kt—B6 Mate.

16. Kt—B7ch.
17. R×Kt B×R
18. Kt—Q4

Playing to bring his superior weight to bear. If 18 B—K2 (against R—Q8ch.), B—QB4.

18. B—Kt3
[Diagram 42]

19. P—B5

The point. He now develops his bishop with good effect through the threat of B—Kt5ch., winning a piece. If in reply 19 . . ., P—QR3; 20 P—

(BLACK) ALEKHINE

(WHITE) ZNOSKO-BOROVSKY

Position before White's 19th move.

(DIAGRAM 42)

B6, P—QKt4 (if B—QB4; 21 P×P, B×Kt; 22 Q×B); 21 P—B7, R—QB1; 22 Kt×Kt P, while if 19 . . ., B×P; 20 B—Kt5ch., K—K2; 21 Kt—Kt3, winning a piece.

19. Kt×P
20. B—Kt5ch. Kt—Q2
21. Q—B3 P—QR3

Now Black's difficulties with his development become apparent for if 21 . . ., B—K2; 22 Q—B7 (preventing O—O), P—QR3; 23 B—R4, P—QKt4; 24 B—Q1, and O—O is still impossible because of 25 Kt—B6.

22. B×Ktch. R×B
23. Q—B8ch.

Preparing to give up a third piece to keep Black tied up. If 23 O—O, at once, Black has a choice of B×P; 24 Q×B, R×Kt; or 23 . . ., P—Kt3;

threatening R×Kt and B—Q B4. While if 23 Kt—B3, B—Q6; 24 Q—B8ch., R—Q1; 25 Q×P, B×P; 26 Q—B6ch., K—K2; and Black obtains a quick deployment of forces.

23.		R—Q1
24.	Q×P	R×Kt
25.	Q—B6ch.	R—Q2
26.	O—O	B—Q6
27.	R×P	

The point of White's 23rd and 24th moves. Black must now exert all his resources to save the game.

27.		B—B4ch.
28.	K—R1	B—Kt4
29.	Q×Pch.	R—K2
30.	R×Rch.	B×R
31.	Q—B8ch.	B—Q1
32.	Q—K6ch.	B—K2

Drawn.

White can hope for no more now, while Black cannot escape perpetual check in his exposed situation, for if 32 . . ., K—B1; some such line follows as 33 Q—B5ch., K—K2; 34 Q—Kt 5ch. (or P—QR4, B×P; 35 Q—Kt4, R—B1; 36 Q—Kt4ch.), K—K3; 35 Q×P, R—K1; 36 P—QR4, B—B3; 37 Q—Kt3, R—B1; 38 Q—Kt3ch., K—Q2; 39 P—K6ch., K—B2; 40 Q—Kt3ch., K—B1; 41 Q—Q3, K—Kt2; 42 Q×KRPch., B—B2; 43 Q—Kt 1ch., K—R2; 44 P—K7.

E. D. Bogolyubov (b. 1889), a Russian by birth, adopted Germany as his country after his internment there during the First World War. He rapidly achieved prominence in the 1920's and his vigorous and aggressive style won him a number of tournaments, notably Moscow, 1925. By 1929 he was regarded as a challenger for the world title, but was soundly defeated twice, in 1929 and 1934.

S. Tartakower (b. 1887), also born in Russia, later took French nationality. An original and aggressive player, he always seeks to escape from the book and this has perhaps cost him a number of prizes. He has, however, won many tournaments, as for example at Liege, 1930, and at Hastings, 1946.

GAME 33

PONZIANI OPENING

TARTAKOWER–BOGOLYUBOV

London tournament, 1927.

1.	P—K4	P—K4
2.	Kt—KB3	Kt—QB3
3.	P—B3	Kt—B3

Stronger and more usual is P—Q4 at once.

4. P—Q4 P—Q4
5. KP×P Q×P
6. B—K2 P—K5

As a result of his choice on the 3rd move Black must now decide between this not very satisfactory move, and 6 . . ., P×P; which leads to positions akin to some in the Danish Gambit or the Goring Gambit, where White gets a strong though not decisive attack at the cost of a pawn.

7. KKt—Q2 P—K6

A sharp move, putting a keen edge on the game. It is not altogether satisfactory, however, for though White's king side is broken up he secures control of the centre.

8. P×P Q×KtP
9. B—B3 Q—R6
10. Q—K2 Kt—KKt5

Preventing 11 Q—Kt2, or 11 B—Kt2, by the threat to the KP.

11. Kt—K4 Q—R5ch.
12. K—Q1

If 12 Kt—Kt3, B—Q3; 13 Q—Kt2, Kt×RP; with advantage.

12. B—Q2

He could retain some say in the centre by 12 . . ., P—B4; 13 B×Kt, P×Kt. White now has time to work his QB round to the K side.

13. B—Q2 O—O—O
14. B—K1 Q—K2

If 14 . . ., Q—R4; 15 P—KR3, and if 14 . . ., Q—R6; 15 Kt—Kt5.

15. B×Kt Q×Kt
16. B—B3 Q—Kt3
17. Kt—Q2 P—B3

Preferring to hold his K4 rather than try and fight it out for his K5 by P—B4.

18. B—Kt3 P—KR4
19. R—KKt1 P—R5
20. B—B2 Q—B2
21. P—K4 B—Q3
22. B—K3 Kt—R4

A rather pointless move. His counterweight to White's centre lies on the other wing.

23. P—Kt4 B—R5ch.
24. K—K1

Safer was K—B1. The king comes under fire on the other flank.

24. Kt—B3
25. Kt—B4 B×RP

[Diagram 43]

A counter-attack just in time, for he was threatened with Kt—Kt2, and if instead 25 . . ., Kt—K2; 26 P—Kt5, B×KtP; 27 Kt×Bch., R×Kt; 28 Q×B, with good chances of a successful storming attack. Of course if now 26 Q×B, Q×Kt; 27 R×P, Q×Pch.; while 26 R—Kt2, B—Kt6ch.; leaves Black reasonably safe.

(BLACK) BOGOLYUBOV

(WHITE) TARTAKOWER

Position before White's 26th move.

(DIAGRAM 43)

26. Kt—Kt2 B×R
27. B×B Kt×QP

He must lose another piece, for if 27 . . ., P—QKt4; 28 Kt ×B, P×Kt; 29 Q—R6ch., K—Q2; 30 B—Kt4ch., and White will have two bishops for rook and pawn. Attack and counter-attack now continue at a fast pace.

28. P×Kt B—B3
29. P—Q5 B×P

He prefers a fighting line, even at the cost of another piece, rather than 29 . . ., B—Q2; 30 R—B1, threatening 31 B—R2, when Black has little hope of saving the game.

30. P×B KR—K1
31. B—K3 P—KB4
32. K—B1 P—KKt4

The likely looking P—B5 will not win the piece because of 33 B—Kt4ch., K—Kt1; 34 B—K6, Q—B3; 35 B—B2. He must therefore stake everything on his K side pawns.

33. Q—KB2 P—Kt5
34. B—R1

If 34 B×KtP, R×B; 35 B×Pch., K—Kt1; 36 Q×R, Q×Bch.; 37 Q—B2 (K—Kt1, R—Kt1ch.; 38 K—R1, Q×Pch.; or 37 K—K1, Q×P; threatening Q—R8ch.), Q—R6 ch.; 38 K—K2 (K—K1, Q—R8ch.), Q—B6; 39 K—B1, Q—R6ch.; drawing.

34. R×P

A surprise, but not the best move. With 34 . . ., P—B5; 35 Q×P (B×P, R—B1), Q×Qch.; 36 B×Q, R—B1; his pawns should give him at least a draw.

35. B—B4

After 35 B×R, Q×B; Black would threaten 36 . . ., P—Kt6; 37 Q—Q2, Q—R8ch.; 38 K—K2, Q×R. The reply 36 B—B4, would allow 36 . . ., P—Kt6; 37 Q—Kt2, Q—Kt4ch.; 38 K—Kt1, R—K7; while 36 Q—B4, would be answered by Q—R8 ch.; 37 B—Kt1, Q—R6ch.; 38 K—B2, P—Kt6ch.; 39 K—B3, Q—R8 Mate.

35. R—K5

Thrill follows thrill now that Black is committed to an all out effort. He must close one of the two bishops' diagonals, for a quiet move such as R(4)—Q1 would allow 36 Q×QRP with a terrific attack.

36. B×R P×B
37. K—Kt1 P—Kt6

Not 37 . . ., R—KB4; 38 Q×QRP, R×B; 39 R—Q1, P—B3; 40 Q—R8ch., K—B2; 41 Q—Q8 Mate.

38. Q—K3 Q—B3
39. R—Kt1 R—KB4

White has consolidated his position, and Black with his material inferiority cannot afford moves like P—Kt3. This attack, however, leads nowhere and now the Black pawns begin to fall.

40. Q×RP R—Q4
41. Q—R8ch. K—Q2
42. Q×P Q—Q5ch.
43. K—R1 P—K6
44. R—QB1

Correct was 44 Q×Pch. first, defending the bishop. Now Black can get out of his difficulties.

44. P—Kt7ch.

The point. White can no longer answer 45 K—R2 because of 45 . . ., Q×Bch.

45. K×P P—R6ch.

Missing his opportunity. After 45 . . ., Q—K5ch.; 46 K—Kt1 (K—R3, Q—B6ch.; 47 K×P, R—R4 Mate or K—B1, Q×Bch.; 47 K—Kt1, Q—Kt6ch.; 48 K—R1, Q—R6ch.; 49 K—Kt1, R—Kt4ch.), R—Kt 4ch.; 47 B×R, Q×Q; 48 B×RP, Q×P; 49 Kt—B4, P—K7; with very good chances. Now it is easy for White.

46. K—B3 K—K3
47. R×P P—R7
48. Q—B6ch. R—Q3

Or 48 . . ., K—B4; 49 R—B7ch.

49. Q—K8ch. Resigns.

For if 49 . . ., K—Q4; 50 Q—R5ch., K—K3; 51 Q—B7 Mate. A titanic struggle from start to finish.

GAME 34

ALEKHINE–CAPABLANCA

22nd match game,
Buenos Aires, 1927.

Pillsbury Attack

1. P—Q4 Kt—KB3
2. P—QB4 P—K3
3. Kt—QB3 P—Q4
4. B—Kt5 B—K2
5. P—K3 O—O
6. Kt—B3 QKt—Q2
7. R—B1 P—B3
8. B—Q3 P×P
9. B×P Kt—Q4
10. B×B Q×B
11. Kt—K4

If 11 O—O, Black frees his game with Kt×Kt; 12 R×Kt, P—K4. The text move, however, leads to a drawish position unless he can play O—O first because of the check on his QKt4.

11. Kt(4)—B3

If Kt(2)—B3 he not only reduces his chances of playing P—K4 or P—QB4 later but his advanced knight would be a target for the White KP.

12. Kt—Kt3 Q—Kt5ch.
13. Q—Q2 Q×Qch.
14. K×Q R—Q1
15. KR—Q1

Better than 15 B—Q3, P—K4; 16 P×P, Kt—Kt5; 17 P—K6, Kt(2)—K4; 18 Kt×Kt, Kt×Kt; 19 P×Pch., K×P; 20 R—B3, P—QKt4; as in the 20th game of the match. Now if 15 . . ., P—K4; 16 K—K2, P×P (P—K5; 17 Kt—Kt5); 17 R×P, with considerable pressure.

15. P—QKt3
16. P—K4

Here K—K2 would not be sufficiently aggressive, Black getting a solid position by 16 . . ., B—Kt2; 17 R—Q2, K—B1; 18 R(B)—Q1, K—K2; 19 P—K4, P—KR3.

16. B—Kt2
17. P—K5 Kt—K1

Against Kt—K4—Q6.

18. K—K3 K—B1

Allowing White to get his knights on aggressive squares. Preferable was P—KR3.

19. Kt—Kt5 P—KR3
20. Kt(5)—K4 K—K2

If 20 . . ., P—QB4; 21 P—B4, P×Pch.; 22 R×P, with by far the freer game.

21. P—B4 P—KB4
22. Kt—B3 Kt—B2

Now P—QB4 would be answered by 23 P—Q5.

23. Kt(Kt)—K2 P—KKt4
24. P—KR4 P—Kt5

P×P would lead to a probable draw after 25 R—KR1, R—KKt1; 26 R×P, R×P; 27 R×P, QR—KKt1; but not 25 . . ., P—B4; 26 R×P, B×P; 27 R—KKt1, R—KKt1; 28 R×P, B—Kt2; 29 R—R7ch., winning a piece.

25. Kt—Kt3 P—QR4
26. B—Kt3 QR—B1

If 26 . . ., P—Kt4; 27 P—Q5 (P—R4, P—Kt5; 28 Kt(B)—K2, QR—B1; 29 R—B2, Kt—Q4ch.; with equality), BP×P (Kt×Pch.; 28 B×Kt, BP×B; 29 Kt×KtP); 28 Kt(B)—K2, QR—B1; 29 Kt—Q4, with positional compensation for the pawn, as in the 24th game of the match.

27. P—R3 R—B1
28. R—Q2 B—R1
29. R(2)—QB2 P—B4

Not 29 . . ., Kt—Q4ch.; 30 Kt×Kt, KP×Kt (forced); 31 B×P. Black now seeks to break out of his constricted position.

30. P × P Kt × P
31. Kt—R4 Kt(2)—R3

Not 31 . . ., Kt × B; 32 R × Ktch., R × R; 33 R × Rch., K—Q1; 34 R—B3, Kt—R8 (Kt—B4; 35 Kt × KtP, winning); 35 Kt × KtP, B—Kt2; 36 Kt—K2, R—B2; 37 Kt—Q4 (threatening R—B1), R—B 2; 38 Kt × Pch., wins.

(BLACK) CAPABLANCA

(WHITE) ALEKHINE

Position before White's 32nd move.

(DIAGRAM 44)

32. B × P

A brilliant effort to force a win. The likely looking 32 Kt × KtP, loses a piece by R—QKt1; 33 Kt × B, R × Bch.

32. K × B
33. Kt × KtP R—QKt1

White threatened P—Kt4.

34. Kt × B R—Kt6ch.

Missing his best chance, which was R × Kt, for any attempt by White to make quick use of his rooks on the QB file leads to an ending in Black's favour, as for example 35 P—Kt4, P × P; 36 P × P, Kt × P; 37 R × Kt, R—R6ch.; 38 R(5)—B3 (K—B2, Kt—Q 6ch.), R × Rch.; 39 R × R, Kt—Q4ch.; or 35 R × Kt, Kt × R; 36 R × Kt, KR—B1; 37 R × R, R × R. White must therefore play 35 R—Q1, a change of file which is less effective when Black can oppose rooks, as he can after 34 . . ., R × Kt, than in the game as played when White controls the file. However, Alekhine suggested R × Kt; 35 Kt—K2, by-passing the dangers.

35. R—B3 R × Rch.
36. P × R R × Kt
37. R—Q1 R—KB1

He must withdraw his king from the defence of the BP, for if Kt—Kt2, the rook comes in at QKt6 after 38 R—QKt1.

38. R—Q6ch. K—K2
39. R × P Kt—B2
40. R—R7ch.

Black threatens Kt—Kt4 or Kt—Q4, but now White is able to force the king back further, since if 40 . . ., R—B2; 41 Kt × Pch.

40. K—Q1
41. P—B4 Kt(2)—K3

Preparing the counter-measure 42 . . ., Kt × P; 43 K × Kt, Kt—K3ch.; 44 K—K 3, P—B5ch.; but White prevents the manœuvre by threatening to exchange off the rooks by R—R8ch. Neverthe-less, the best reply was 42 Kt—K2.

42.	R—R7	Kt—B2
43.	R×P	Kt(4)—K3
44.	P—R5	K—Q2

Still not Kt×P; 45 K×Kt, Kt—K3ch.; 46 K—K3, P—B5ch.; 47 K—K4, P×Kt; 48 R—R8ch.

45.	P—R6	Kt×P
46.	K×Kt	Kt—K3ch.
47.	K—K3	P—B5ch.
48.	K—B2	P×Ktch.
49.	K×P	R—KR1
50.	R—Q5ch.	K—K2

Not K—B3; 51 R—Q6ch. Black's defence against White's widely spread pawns has to be extremely exact. Fortunately for him each one is isolated.

51.	P—B5	R×P
52.	P—B6	Kt—B1
53.	R—B5	K—Q1
54.	K×P	R—Kt3ch.
55.	K—B3	K—B2
56.	P—Kt4	Kt—K3
57.	R—Q5	Kt—B1

Better than K×P; 58 R—Q6ch., K—Kt4; 59 K—K3, and Black's two pieces are completely tied up, since he dare not risk 59 . . ., Kt—B1; 60 R×R, Kt×R; and the pawns cannot be held.

58.	R—B5	Kt—K3
59.	R—Q5	Kt—B1
60.	R—R5	

Fighting for a win, but now the pawns begin to fall.

60.		R×BP
61.	K—K4	R—B8
62.	R—R7ch.	K—B3
63.	R—R6ch.	K—Q2
64.	R—R7ch.	K—K3
65.	R—R6ch.	K—K2
66.	P—R4	Kt—Q2
67.	R—R6	

After R—R5, to prevent Kt—B4ch. and also the loss of the KP, Black can play K—K3.

67.		R—K8ch.
68.	K—Q4	Kt×P
69.	P—R5	Kt×P
70.	R—R7ch.	K—Q3
71.	P—R6	R—QR8
72.	P—R7	Kt—B3
73.	R—QKt7	Kt—Q2
74.	R—Kt2	

Bowing to the inevitable and admitting that he cannot win. Now, Black in turn tries to win, but his hope is a forlorn one for it must depend on a White blunder.

74.		R×P
75.	R—Q2	Kt—B4
76.	K—B4 dis. ch.	K—B3
77.	R—KR2	R—R5ch.
78.	K—B3	R—KKt5
79.	K—Q2	R—Kt6
80.	R—R5	K—Kt4
81.	K—K2	K—B5
82.	R—R4ch.	K—B6
83.	K—B2	R—Q6
84.	R—KB4	K—Q7
85.	K—Kt2	R—Q4
86.	K—B3	K—Q6

Drawn.

A. Nimzowitch (1886–1935), a Russian who adopted Denmark as his native country, first came into prominence early in the twentieth century. His style was so unusual that for a time he was regarded as a Hypermodern, but in fact he was an original thinker and iconoclast and became a great teacher. He was always highly placed in tournaments, his best result being the 1st prize at Carlsbad, 1929, but never obtained the match for the world title to which he was generally regarded as entitled.

GAME 35

CAPABLANCA–NIMZOWITCH

Kissingen tournament, 1928.

NIMZO-INDIAN DEFENCE

1. P—Q4 Kt—KB3
2. P—QB4 P—K3
3. Kt—QB3 B—Kt5
4. Q—B2 P—Q4
5. B—Kt5

A move proved inferior for the first time in this game. Black's play, holding the gambit pawn, leads to a great battle.

5. P×P
6. Kt—B3 P—Kt4
7. P—QR4 P—B3
8. B×Kt

Not P—K3 because he wants to take advantage of Black's weakness on the long diagonal.

8. P×B

If Q×B; 9 P×P, P×P; 10 Q—K4, with a position sufficient to deter Black from trying the line, though Alekhine subsequently suggested the brilliant continuation 10 . . ., Q—Kt3; 11 Q×R, Q—B7; 12 Q×Kt, O—O; and Black must recover his rook with a strong game.

9. P—KKt3 P—QR3

Beginning an unexpected manœuvre, as a result of which White's bishop on the long diagonal will bite on thin air.

10. B—Kt2 R—R2
11. O—O R—Q2
12. Q—B1 O—O
13. Q—R6 B×Kt

The alternative answer to the threat of Kt—K4 fails by 13 . . ., K—R1; 14 Kt—K4, B—K2; 15 Kt(3)—Kt5, P×Kt; 16 Kt—B6, B×Kt; 17 B—K4. The text move frees the White knight from the defence of his QP, but it remains without much future even so.

14. P×B K—R1
15. Kt—Q2 P—KB4
16. KR—Kt1

If now 16 P—K4, P—K4; and the White centre goes to pieces

after 17 KP×P, R—Q3; 18 Q—K3, P×P; 19 P×P, R×P; 20 Kt—B3, R—Q6. Now White threatens 17 Kt×P, P×Kt; 18 R×Kt, making Black's extra pawn valueless.

16. P—K4

Now if 17 Kt×P, P×P; 18 P×P, R×P; 19 Kt—K5, R—Q3; 20 Q—B1, Q—B3; 21 Q—B3, R—K3.

17. Kt—B3 R—Q3
18. Q—K3

He must try and hold what centre he has, for if 18 Q—R5, P×P; 19 Kt—Kt5, P—R3; 20 Kt×Pch., R×Kt; 21 Q×R, P×P; and the Black pawns will win.

18. P—K5
19. Kt—Q2 Kt—Q2
20. P—Kt4

A fighting reply. A less aggressive line would lead to slow suffocation. Now the game becomes very critical.

20. Kt—B3
21. P×BP B×P

The natural move and good enough, but more decisive was 21 . . ., Kt—Q4; 22 Q—R3 (Q×P, Kt×P), Kt—B5; 23 Q—K3, Q—Kt4; 24 Q×P (forced), B×P; winning.

22. Q—B4 Q—Q2
23. B×P

The only way to get freedom in the centre, for if 23 Kt×KP, B×Kt; 24 B×B, R—Kt1ch.; 25 B—Kt2 (K—R1, R—Kt5), Kt—Q4; 23 Q—K5ch, (Q—B3, R(3)—Kt3), P—B3; 27 Q—R5, Kt—B5; winning.

23. Kt×B
24. Kt×Kt R—Kt3ch.
25. Kt—Kt3

The climax of Black's play, for White must now lose the exchange. If 25 K—R1 (K—B1, B×Kt; 26 Q×B, Q—R 6ch.), Q—Q4 (not R—Kt5; 26 Kt—B6); 26 P—B3, R—K1; threatening 27 . . ., R×Kt; 28 P×R, B×P; winning easily.

25. B×R
26. R×B P—KB4

Threatening R—Kt5 followed by P—B5.

27. P—B3 Q—KKt2

But now Black begins to go wrong, curiously enough in the same way as Mieses did against Capablanca in Game 28, by not forcing exchanges after obtaining a material advantage. Better was 27 . . ., Q—Q3.

28. K—B2 Q—B3
29. P×P BP×P

A further error, for though the pawns look strong, White has now a passed pawn which enables him to fight back with magnificent virtuosity.

[Diagram 45]

30. R—Q1 K—Kt1
31. P—Q5 Q×P

A final misjudgment; Q—Q3 was essential. The full subtlety

(BLACK) NIMZOWITCH

(WHITE) CAPABLANCA

Position before White's 30th move.

(DIAGRAM 45)

of White's recovery has still to appear.

32. P—Q6 Q—B3
33. P—Q7 P—B6
34. Kt×P P—B7

Of course not Q×Kt; 35 Q×Q, R×Q; 36 P—Q8=Qch., nor R—Kt4; 35 R—Q5, R×Kt; 36 R×R, Q—Kt3ch.; 37 K—Kt2, R×R; 38 Q×R.

35. R—Q6

A big surprise. The tame 35 R—QB1, would lose by 35 . . ., R—Kt4 (not Q—Kt3ch.; 36 Q—Q4); 36 P—K4, Q—Kt 3ch.

35. Q—Q1

Threatening R×R and still anticipating a won game. Other lines lead only to a probable draw; for example, 35 . . ., Q×R; 36 Kt×Q, R×Q; 37 P—Q8=Qch., R—B1; 38 Q—B7, R×Kt; 39 Q×P, or 35 . . ., P—B8=Q; 36 Q×Q, Q×Kt; 37 P—Q8=Q, R×Q; 38 R×R(8)ch. White uses his passed pawn with magnificent effect, so that Black's move is the most reasonable one.

36. Q—K5 R×Kt

Of course not 36 . . ., P—B8=Q; 37 R×Rch., P×R; 38 Q—Kt7 Mate. The text appears finally to break White's attack, but there is more to it.

37. Q—K8ch.

The point. Of course 37 Q×R would lose. Now if 37 . . ., K—Kt2; 38 R×Rch., P×R; 39 Q×Q, P—B8=Q; 40 Q—K 7ch., K—R3; 41 P—Q8=Q, and White actually wins, so Black must submit to the draw by perpetual check.

37. R—B1
38. R×Rch. Drawn.

M. Euwe (b. 1901), the Dutch master, won the world championship from Alekhine in 1935, only to lose it again two years later. A player of deep and accurate positional sense, he has persistently won prizes in master tournaments, though often just failing to win the 1st prize. One of his best results was his 1st prize at London, 1946. (Pronunciation :—Erver.)

GAME 36

EUWE–BOGOLYUBOV

8th match game, 1928.

PILLSBURY ATTACK

1. P—Q4 P—Q4
2. P—QB4 P—K3
3. Kt—QB3 Kt—KB3
4. B—Kt5 QKt—Q2
5. P—K3 P—B3
6. P—QR3

Preventing the Cambridge Springs Defence.

6. B—K2
7. Kt—B3 Kt—K5
8. B×B Q×B
9. Q—B2 P—KB4

A solid variation in which he will labour under the permanent disadvantages of weak Black squares and a confined bishop.

10. B—K2 O—O
11. O—O R—B3

P—K4 is impossible because of the loss of the QP, and if first 11 . . ., Kt×Kt ; then 12 Q×Kt, again prevents P—K4.

12. Kt—K5

A double-edged move. He permanently prevents P—K4 but has to allow some weakening of his position on the K side. The more orthodox play would be to operate on the Q side by P—B5 and P—QKt4—Kt5.

12. QKt×Kt
13. P×Kt R—R3
14. P—KKt3

To prevent Q—R5. Were he to permit Q—R5 and then play P—R3, Black could at once continue with P—KKt4—Kt5.

14. B—Q2
15. P—B3 Kt×P

A bold sacrifice designed to take advantage of the weakness White has permitted. But probably a quieter line like Kt—Kt4 would in the end have proved more effective.

16. P×Kt Q—Kt4
17. K—Kt2

If K—B2, then R—R7ch. ; 18 K—K1, Q×KP ; 19 P—B4, Q×Pch.

17. R—Kt3
18. P—KKt4 Q×P
19. P—B4 P×KtP

To prevent 20 P—Kt5 and 21 B—R5.

20. Q—Q3 Q—Kt3
21. P—Kt4

Preparing for 22 R—R1 with the threat of 23 R×P, K×R; 24 R—R1ch., K—Kt1; 25 Q×R. White is now beginning to recover the initiative.

21. R—KB1
22. P—QB5 Q—Q1
23. Q—Kt3 P—KR4
24. R—R1 R—R3
25. QR—KB1 P—QKt3

Black is entirely without prospects unless he can open some more lines.

26. Q—R4 Q—R1
27. B—Q3 P—R4
28. Q—Kt5 B—K1

If RP×P; 29 R×P, R×R; 30 Q×R, R—B1 (against 31 B—R7ch.); 31 RP×P, with a great advantage.

29. R—R1

Black's manœuvre has succeeded in making White halt his initiative. If 29 Kt—R4, RP×P; 30 Kt×P, Q×P; with good chances.

29. Q—Kt1
30. KtP×P

This fails to keep Black contained. It was based on the line 30 ..., P×RP; 31 QR—QKt1, Q—R2; 32 Kt—R4 (not R—Kt6, P—QR5), and Black cannot get out. Better was 30 KR—QKt1 (not QR—QKt1, RP×P; 31 RP×P, P×P; 32 P×P, Q—R2), Q—R2; 31 Kt—R4, P—Kt4; 32 Kt—B3, and White holds the Q side.

30. P—Kt4
31. Kt—K2 Q—R2
32. Kt—Kt3

He cannot prevent Black's queen coming back into the game, for if KR—QB1, Q×RP; threatening Q—Q7.

32. Q×BP
33. P—B5

If Kt×P, B×Kt; 34 R×B, Q—K6; 35 R×R, Q—B6ch.; with a draw by perpetual check. If 35 Q×P, R×R; 36 Q×R, Q×B; wins.

33. P—R5

(BLACK) BOGOLYUBOV

(WHITE) EUWE

Position before White's 34th move.

(DIAGRAM 46)

34. R×P

A most critical position, with

both players on the attack. If White here tries to continue his attack at once with P—B6, Black plays P—R6ch.; 35 K—B1 (not K—R2, Q—KB7 Mate), R(3)×Pch.; 36 P×R, R×Pch.; 37 K—K2 (K—K1, Q—B6ch.; 38 K—K2, Q—Kt7ch.; 39 K—K3 ?, R—B6 Mate), Q—KB7ch.; 38 K—Q1, Q×Kt; and White will have difficulty in saving the game. Alternatively in this variation, if White tries 35 R×P, then P×Rch.; 36 K—R1, R—B2; 37 P×P, Q—KB7; 38 Kt—K2 (R—KKt1, P—R7; 39 R—Kt2, Q—K8 ch.; wins), Q—Kt7ch.; 39 Q×Q, P×Qch.; 40 K×P, R×Pch.; wins. Nor is 34 Q×KtP any better, for then P×Kt; 35 R×R, Q—KB7ch.; 36 K—R1, P—Kt7ch.; 37 Q×P, Q×Qch.; 38 K×Q, P×R; 39 R—R1, P—R4; 40 P—B6, P—B4; 41 P—R6, P—B5; 42 B—Kt6 (P—R7, B—B3), B—B3; 43 R×P, P—Q5 dis. ch.; wins. Probably best is simply 34 Kt—K2, P—Q5; 35 Kt—B4, Q—B6; 36 P—B6, Q—Q7ch.; 37 K—B1, R—B2; 38 Q×KtP, P—B4. The text, which looks strong, has one small flaw.

34. R×R
35. P—B6

If Q×R, Q—K6; 36 Q×P, Q×B; 37 P—B6, and Black must take a perpetual check, or Q×KP is dangerous.

35. R—R7ch.

Resolving the problem by force.

36. K×R Q—KB7ch.

Drawn.

Not 37 K—R1, Q—B6ch.; 38 K—Kt1, Q×Ktch.; 39 K—B1, Q×Bch.; 40 K—K1, Q—R2; wins. A very keen-edged battle.

M. Vidmar (b. 1885), of Yugoslav nationality, came into prominence early in the twentieth century and was for thirty years a consistent prizewinner in master tournaments, though seldom winning a 1st prize. His victory at Bad Sliac, 1932, was one of his best results.

GAME 37

VIDMAR–EUWE

Carlsbad tournament, 1929.

QUEEN'S PAWN GAME

1. P—Q4 Kt—KB3
2. Kt—KB3 P—KKt3
3. B—Kt5

An unorthodox development of the bishop which almost inevitably leads to giving up the bishop for the knight.

3.		B—Kt2
4.	QKt—Q2	P—B4
5.	P—K3	

If P—K4, Black will control the long diagonal.

5.		P—Kt3
6.	B—Q3	B—Kt2
7.	O—O	P—KR3
8.	B—KB4	P—Q3
9.	P—B3	Kt—R4
10.	Q—Kt3	

White allows a certain amount of disruption in his pawn position to obtain open lines for his pieces. The safe 10 B—Kt3, Kt×B; 11 RP× Kt, offered fewer possibilities.

10.		Kt×B
11.	P×Kt	O—O

If P×P; 12 Kt×P, and Black can only give White an isolated pawn at the cost of his valuable KB. White cannot answer the text move with 12 B×P, because of P—B5, followed by P—Q4.

12.	QR—Q1	Kt—B3
13.	B—Kt1	

Now B×P would be answered by Kt—R4.

13.		P×P
14.	P×P	P—K3

Black cannot have the threat of B×P hanging over him indefinitely, but now his QP is weak.

15.	Kt—K4	Kt—K2

P—Q4 would allow White to establish himself strongly on his K5.

16.	Q—R3	Kt—B4
17.	R—Q2	Q—K2
18.	Kt—Kt3	Kt×Kt
19.	BP×Kt	KR—B1
20.	P—KKt4	R—B2
21.	P—B5	KP×P
22.	P×P	P—KKt4
23.	R—K1	Q—B3

The immediate disruption of his K side pawns has been averted, and he threatens P—Kt5, winning the knight.

24.	P—R3	QR—QB1
25.	R(Q)—Q1	

Of course if 25 Q×RP, B×Kt. White is now on the defensive and Black's superior development begins to tell. Somewhat better was R(Q)—K2, and if R—B8; 26 R—K8ch., R×R; 27 R×R.

25.		R—B5
26.	P—Q5	

He can no longer stand the threat of B×Kt.

26.		P—QR4

It was better to play for equality with Q×KtP; for then 27 Q×RP, B—R1 (B×P; 28 R×B, R—B8; 29 B—Q3, R×Rch.; 30 Kt×R, Q—B8; 31 Q—K7, B—B6; 32 K—B1, Q—B5ch.; with nothing more than perpetual check); 28 Q—Q7 (not B—Q3, R(5)—B2; 29 Q—R4, B×P), R—B8; 29

R×R (not R—K8ch., B—B1), R×R; 30 Q—K8ch. (B—Q3, R×Rch.; 31 Kt×R, Q—B8; 32 Q—K8ch., B—B1; 33 Q×B, Q×Ktch.), K—R2; 31 P—B6 dis. ch., Q×B; 32 P×B, R×Rch.; 33 Kt×R, K×P; and a draw is almost certain.

27.	Kt—Q2	Q—Q5ch.
28.	K—R1	Q×QP

Better was simply R(5)—B2; 29 Kt—K4, Q×KtP; 30 Q×QP, but Black sees mating possibilities by means of a combinative assault on the White king.

(BLACK) EUWE

(WHITE) VIDMAR

Position before White's 29th move.

(DIAGRAM 47)

29.	B—K4	R×B
30.	Kt×R	Q×BP
31.	Kt×QP	B×Pch.
32.	K×B	R—B7ch.
33.	K—R1	Q—B5

The key to Black's combination. An apparently inescapable mate on the move is threatened, but White has seen further and now brings his own still more beautiful combination into effect.

34.	R—K8ch.	B—B1

Clearly not K—R2; 35 Q—Q3ch.

35.	R×Bch.	K×R

Of course if K—Kt2; 36 R×Pch.

36.	Kt—B5dis. ch.	K—Kt1
37.	Q—B8ch.	Resigns.

It is mate next move. A galling resignation when he is still left threatening his own mate on the move. For this exquisite piece of play Vidmar was awarded a brilliancy prize.

GAME 38

ALEKHINE–BOGOLYUBOV

11th match game, Weisbaden, 1929.

PILLSBURY ATTACK

1.	P—Q4	Kt—KB3
2.	P—QB4	P—B3
3.	Kt—QB3	P—K3
4.	Kt—B3	P—Q4
5.	B—Kt5	QKt—Q2
6.	P—K4	

A bold method of avoiding

the Cambridge Springs Defence.

6. P×KP
7. Kt×P Q—Kt3

Q—R4ch., would avoid the break-up of his K side pawns.

8. Kt×Ktch. P×Kt
9. B—B1 P—K4
10. B—Q3

Sacrificing a pawn to secure open lines for his bishops and rooks.

10. P×P
11. O—O B—K2

He has no time for P—QB4, for then 12 R—K1ch., B—K2; 13 Q—K2, Q—Q1 (Q—Q3; 14 B—B4); 14 B—R6 and the threat of B—Kt7 followed by B ×BP ties up Black completely.

12. R—K1 Kt—B1
13. Kt—R4 B—K3
14. Kt—B5 B—Kt5

Hoping to castle on the Q side with a good game.

15. Kt—Kt7ch. K—Q2
16. R—K4 R—KKt1
17. Kt—R5 B—K2
[Diagram 48]

18. P—QKt4

Black has now somewhat consolidated his position, so White gives up a second pawn to keep the pot boiling. It is rare to get such a tense situation so early in a Queen's Pawn opening.

18. P—KB4
19. P—B5 Q×KtP

(BLACK) BOGOLYUBOV

(WHITE) ALEKHINE

Position before White's 18th move.

(DIAGRAM 48)

He has now no option but to accept the offer. If Q—B2; 20 B—KB4, Q—B1; 21 R×Pch.

20. R—K5

Better than 20 R—Kt1, Q×P; 21 R×KtPch., K—B1; 22 B—QR6, P×R; 23 R—Kt5 dis. ch., K—Q1; 24 R×Q, B×R; and Black has a good game.

20. Kt—Kt3

Not liking P—B3; 21 R—Kt1, Q—R4; 22 R×Pch., K—K1 (K—B1; 23 KR×B, Kt×R; 24 R×B); 23 KR×B, Kt×R; 24 B×P, Kt—B1; 25 Q—K2.

21. R—Kt1 Q—R4

If Q×R; 22 B×Q, Kt×R; 23 Q×Pch., with advantage.

22. R—K2 P—Kt3

Of course not B×BP; 23 Kt—B6ch. nor B×RP; 23 B×Pch.

23. P×P P×P
24. R(K)—Kt2 QR—Kt1
25. B—B1 P—B4

By careful play Black has now practically consolidated his position again and his extra pawns begin to look formidable, so White plans to open the QKt file thus deriving what advantage he can from his superior development.

26. P—QR4 K—B2
27. R—Kt5 Q—R1
28. P—R5 P×P
29. B—Q2 R×R

If P—R5; 30 R—R5, Q—B3; 31 B—QKt5, with a strong attack against the exposed king. Black rightly considers that a lead of two pawns is sufficient.

30. R×R R—Kt1
31. R×P Q—Kt2
32. Q—R4 B—Q2
33. Q—R2 Q—Kt6
34. R—R7ch. K—Q3

Not K—B1; 35 B—R6ch., K—Q1; 36 B—R5ch., K—K1; 37 Q×Q, R×Q; 38 R—R8ch.

35. Q—R6ch. R—Kt3
36. Q—R5 R—Kt2
37. R—R6ch. B—B3
38. Kt—Kt7 Q—Q4

Another stage of consolidation is achieved. The king is covered and a White bishop tied down by a mating threat.

39. P—B3

There is nothing in 39 Kt—K8ch., K—Q2.

39. K—Q2

But here Black misses a chance of shutting in the White bishop and opening for his own use the diagonal which White has been forced to weaken. P—Q6 was much better and would prevent White's next move.

40. B—Q3 B—Q1

And here Kt—R5, defending the pawn and threatening a dangerous attack by Kt×Pch., was more promising.

41. Q—R1 Kt—K2

To prevent Kt×P followed by B—K4, but Kt—R5 was still a better move.

42. Kt×P

The first pawn is recovered elegantly. Black cannot answer with Kt×Kt, for then 43 B—K4, winning.

42. Q—Kt6
43. Q—KB1 Kt—Q4
44. R—R1

If 44 B—QB4, Q—Kt8; and White cannot continue with 45 B×Kt, in the hope of B×B; 46 R—Q6ch., because of 45 . . ., Q×Qch.; 46 K×Q, B—Kt 4ch.

44. B—QKt4
45. B×Bch. Q×B
46. Q—K1

Black has succeeded in simplifying the position and is still a pawn ahead, so White now switches his attack suddenly to the other flank.

46.		Q—B3
47.	Q—Kt3	Q—KKt3
48.	Q—R3	K—B3

(BLACK) BOGOLYUBOV

(WHITE) ALEKHINE

Position before White's 49th move.

(DIAGRAM 49)

49. Kt×Pch.

And with a brilliant stroke he recovers the second pawn. The combination is delightfully contrived.

49.		P×Kt
50.	Q—B8ch.	B—B2
51.	R—B1ch.	Kt—B6

If K—Kt3; 52 B—R5ch., K ×B; 53 Q×R, threatening both R—R1 Mate and Q×Kt.

52. B×Kt R—Kt8

Not P×B; 53 R×Pch., K—Kt3; 54 R—Kt3ch., preventing Q—Kt8ch. and winning the rook.

53. Q—R8ch.

Not yet B—Q2, for then R×Rch.; 54 B×R, Q—Kt8.

53.		K—Q2
54.	Q—R4ch.	K—B1
55.	B—Q2	R×Rch.
56.	B×R	Q—Q3

If Q—Kt8; 57 Q—K8ch., B—Q1 (K—Kt2; 58 Q—K 4ch.); 58 Q—B6ch. The game is now an inevitable draw. No world championship match ever produced a finer struggle than this.

57.	Q—K8ch.	K—Kt2
58.	Q—Kt5ch.	K—R2
59.	Q—R4ch.	K—Kt2
60.	Q—Kt5ch.	B—Kt3
61.	Q—Q3	Q—Kt3
62.	Q×Q	BP×Q
63.	K—B2	K—B3

Drawn.

R. Spielmann (1883–1942) was another of the young masters who began to make a name for themselves early in the twentieth century. In style he was a romantic and reverted to the gambits of an earlier age. His greatest success was winning the big tournament at Semmering, 1926. He was an Austrian.

G. Stoltz (b. 1910) is a young Swedish player who first appeared about 1930 and was at once successful in international competitions.

GAME 39

SPIELMANN–STOLTZ

Bled tournament, 1931.

QUEEN'S GAMBIT

1. P—Q4 P—Q4
2. Kt—KB3 Kt—KB3
3. P—B4 P×P
4. P—K3 P—K3
5. B×P P—B4
6. O—O Kt—B3
7. Kt—B3 P—QR3
8. Q—K2 B—K2

A move generally deferred in order to avoid losing a move with the bishop.

9. P×P B×P
10. P—QR3 Q—B2
11. P—QKt4 B—Q3
12. B—Kt2 Kt—K4
13. Kt×Kt

Initiating a plan to reinforce the advantage of a move which he has already gained.

13. B×Kt
14. P—B4 B×Kt

If B—Q3; 15 Q—B3, threatening P—K4—K5 with a fine game.

15. B×B P—QKt4
16. B×Kt

The point. Black must submit to the disruption of his K side pawns.

16. Q×B
17. Q—B3

If 17 Q×Q, P×Q; 18 B×P, R—KKt1; 19 B—K5, B—Kt 2; 20 R—B2, R—QB1; White, though a pawn up, would have diminished winning chances because of the bishops of opposite colours.

17. Q—Q4
18. P—K4 Q—B3
19. B×P R—KKt1
20. B—K5 B—Kt2
21. KR—K1

White has won the first round. He is a pawn ahead and Black's king is fixed in the centre. Black, however, has some compensation in his pressure on the long diagonal and his control of the QB file.

21. R—QB1
22. QR—Q1

Not 22 QR—B1, Q×R; 23 R×Q, R×Rch.; 24 K—B2, R—B7ch.; 25 K—K3, R(1) ×P; with advantage.

22. Q—B7
23. P—Kt3 R—Kt3

To prevent an attack by B—B6, which in conjunction with the doubling of the rooks on the Q file would threaten mate on his Q1.

24. P—B5 P×P
25. Q×P Q—B3

B—B6 is again threatened. The inability of White's KP to advance owing to his weakness on the long diagonal is now a powerful counter-weight to the extra pawn.

26. Q—B4 Q—K3
27. R—Q6 Q—Kt5
28. Q—B5

White is prepared to allow the exchange of queens only if he can get his KP on to the B file. If Black replies Q×Q; 29 P×Q, R×R; 30 B×R dis. ch., K—Q1; 31 B—B5, and the threat of R—K7 is difficult to meet.

28. R—QB3
29. R—Q2 B—B1
30. Q—B2 Q—Kt4
31. R—KB1

Correct was B—B4. The text move, which looks strong, leaves the KP undefended and after Black's reply there is no more than a draw in the game. Of course Black will not fall into Q×B; 32 Q×P Mate.

31. Q—K2
32. Q—B4 R—Kt5
33. Q—B2 R(5)—Kt3

Forced by the threat of B—B6.

34. Q—Q4 R—B5
35. Q—B2 B—R6

(BLACK) STOLTZ

(WHITE) SPIELMANN

Position before White's 36th move.

(DIAGRAM 50)

36. Q—B4

Now if 36 B—B6, R×B; 37 Q×R, B×R; 38 Q×Qch., K×Q; 39 K×B, R×P; draws easily. White is not prepared to forgo his attempts to win and evolves a plan based upon drawing the bishop from its present diagonal by sacrificing the rook.

36. B×R
37. B—B6 B—R6

For if now Q×B (R×B; 38 Q—Kt8ch., is worse); 38 Q—Kt8ch., K—K2 (R—B1 is no longer possible); 39 Q—Q8ch., K—K3; 40 Q—Q6 Mate. But Black's subtle counter is to allow White to carry through the plan he has played for.

38. R—Q8ch.

Not B×Q, R—B8ch.; 39 K—B2, R—B8ch.; 40 K—K3, R×Q; 41 P×R, K×B; winning a piece.

38. K×R

Q×R; 39 B×Q, leads to identical positions.

39. B×Qch. K×B
40. Q—R4ch. R—B3
41. Q×B

And now at the end of it all Black has proved the more cunning and has the superior position. White, however, is still full of fight.

41. R—QB8ch.
42. K—Kt2 R—QB7ch.
43. K—Kt1 R—Q3

By means of this mating threat Black will be able to double rooks on the 7th rank.

44. Q—R5 K—B1

Not R (3)—Q7 at once because of 45 Q—K5ch., K—Q2 (K—B1; 46 Q—R8ch.); 46 Q—B5ch., K—B3; 47 Q—B6ch., and Black can only avoid perpetual check by withdrawing his rook; for example, 47 . . ., K—Kt2; 48 Q×Pch., K—Kt3; 49 Q—B6ch., R—B3; 50 Q—R1.

45. Q—B3 R(3)—Q7
46. Q—B1 K—Kt1

If R×P, he no longer threatens mate in one and White can play 47 Q—B6, K—Kt1; 48 Q—Q8ch., K—Kt2; 49 Q—Kt5ch., drawing.

47. P—KR4 P—KR4
48. P—K5 R—K7
49. P—K6 P×P

A last trap. If R×P; 50 Q—Q1, R(3)—K7; 51 Q—Q8ch., K—R2; 52 Q—Q3ch., K—R3; 53 Q—Q6ch., R—K3; 54 Q—Q1, with perpetual check.

50. K—R1

All White's other moves are exhausted, for if Q—Q1, then R—Kt7ch.; 51 K—R1, R—R7ch.; 52 K—Kt1, R(B)—Kt7ch.; 53 K—B1, R—R8ch.

50. R—B7
51. Q—KKt1

Again forced because of the same continuation.

51. K—B2
Resigns.

White is in *zugswang*. An exciting game.

E. Colle (1897–1932) was a brilliant Belgian master, whose name is particularly associated with the form of the Queen's Pawn Game named after him. He won the International tournaments at Meran, 1926, and Scarborough, 1927, and 1930.

I. Kashdan (b. 1911) is a young American master who scored an exceptional series of successes in the early 1930's, notably the 1st prizes at Gyor, 1930, and Stockholm, 1930.

GAME 40

COLLE–KASHDAN

Bled tournament, 1931.

COLLE SYSTEM

1. P—Q4 P—Q4
2. Kt—KB3 Kt—KB3
3. P—K3 P—B4
4. P—B3 P—K3
5. QKt—Q2 Kt—B3
6. B—Q3 B—Q3
7. O—O O—O
8. P×P B×P
9. P—K4

The key move of Colle's own system of attack.

9. Q—B2
10. P×P

Though this gives Black an isolated pawn, it is not consistent with the scheme of attack, which requires the use of the square K4. Better was 10 Q—K2 followed by R—K1.

10. P×P
11. Kt—Kt3 B—Kt3
12. Q—B2 R—K1
13. B—KKt5 Kt—K5
14. QR—K1 B—KB4
15. B—K3

White's QKt and QB are unusually ineffective as a result of his 10th move.

15. B—Kt3
16. Kt—R4

(BLACK) KASHDAN

(WHITE) COLLE

Position before Black's 16th move.

(DIAGRAM 51)

16. Kt×KBP

Black tries to force the issue

brilliantly before White can recover. The immediate threat is Kt×B, and if White tries to counter this threat by removing Black's QB, Black wins either by 17 KB×B, Kt—KKt5; 18 B×BPch. (B×RPch., K—R1; 19 Kt—B3, Kt×B), K—R1; 19 Kt—B3, R×B; or by 17 Kt ×B, Kt—KKt5; 18 P—Kt3, Kt×B. An attempt to avoid the mating threats in the above variations by 17 QB×B equally fails after 17 . . ., Q×B; 18 B×B, Kt—Q6 dis. ch.; 19 K—R1, Kt×R; or 18 Q×Kt, Q×Qch.; 19 K×Q, B×B; 20 R×Rch., R×R; 21 R—K1, R×R; 22 K×R, B—Kt8. White must therefore take the knight and if 17 Q×Kt (K×Kt, Q—B5ch.; wins), QB×B; 18 B×B, Q×B; 19 R×Rch., R×R; with advantage. The text reply is the only one by which he can hold the piece, but it involves his king in considerable dangers.

17.	B×Kt	B×Bch.
18.	K×B	Q—Kt3ch.
19.	K—Kt3	R—K6ch.
20.	R×R	Q×Rch.
21.	R—B3	Q—Kt4ch.
22.	K—R3	Kt—K4
23.	R—Kt3	Q—R3
24.	B—B5	

Not B×B, RP×B; and Black threatens to recover the piece by P—KKt4. White has at last succeeded in holding his piece, but his position is far from happy.

24. R—K1

He wants to renew his attempts to recover the piece by B—R4, P—KKt4 and B—Kt3, but if B—R4 at once, 25 Q—Q2 would clear the air for White.

25. Kt—Q4

To free the queen from the defence of the bishop.

25. B—R4

(BLACK) KASHDAN

(WHITE) COLLE

Position before White's 26th move.

(DIAGRAM 52)

26. Q—B2

The situation is extremely difficult and White is very nearly in *zugswang*. For instance, if 26 B—Kt4, B×Bch.; 27 R×B, Kt×R; 28 K×Kt, R—K5ch.; coming out the exchange ahead, and if 26 Kt(Q)—B3, B×Kt; 27 P×B, P—KKt4. The text move, however, does nothing to ease his game, and the only line that promised anything was 26 B×Pch., restoring material equality. Black cannot reply 26 . . ., Q×B; 27 Q×Qch., K×Q; 28 Kt(R)—B5, and White has the advantage; he must therefore play 26 . . ., K—B1. Now not 27 B—B5, P—KKt4; nor 27 Kt(Q)—B5, Q—B5 (threatening B—Kt5ch.); but 27 Q—B5, with good chances. He never has the same opportunity again.

26. P—KKt4
27. B×Pch.

The piece must be returned as K—B1 cannot be prevented. White therefore decides to make sure that he gets his pawn back in exchange for it.

27. K—B1

Taking the sting out of White's last move, and much better than the immediate recovery of the piece either by K×B; 28 Q—B5ch., B—Kt3; 29 Q×KtP, or by Q×B; 28 R×Pch. Now White's reply is forced by the threat of P—Kt5ch.

28. B—B5 P×Kt
29. R—K3 R—K2

A beautiful move, to prevent White capturing the rook with a check, and so threatening Kt—Kt3. For example if in reply 30 Q—K1, then Kt—Kt3; 31 R×R, Kt—B5ch.; 32 K×P, B—K7dis. ch.; 33 K—Kt3, Q—Kt4ch.; 34 K—B2, Q—R5ch.; 35 P—Kt3, Q×RPch.; 36 K—K3, Kt—Kt7ch. Nor does protection of his KB4 help White, for if 30 Kt—K2, then B×Kt; 31 R×B (Q×B, Kt—Q6), Kt—Q6; 32 Q—B3, R×R; 33 Q×R, Kt—B5ch. He therefore plays to remove the double threat to his K3 when the Black knight moves, even though it costs him the exchange.

30. R—K1 B—Kt5ch.

Another fine move which forces the exchange of queens, without which the game would still be difficult to win.

31. B×B Kt—Q6
32. Q×P Kt—B5ch.
33. K—Kt3 Q×Qch.
34. K×Q Kt×Pch.
35. K—Kt5 R×R

The end of a fine combination, and virtually the end of a fine combinative game.

36. P—KR4 Kt—K6
37. B—B3 Kt—B5
38. Kt—B5 R—Kt8ch.
39. K—B4 R—KB8
40. Kt—K3 R—B7
41. Kt—Q1 R—R7
42. P—R5 Kt×P
43. Kt—K3 Kt—Q6ch.
44. K—Kt3 R×QRP
45. Kt×P R—Kt7
46. P—R6 Kt—K4
47. K—B4 Kt—Kt3ch.
48. K—K4 P—Kt3
49. Kt—B6 Kt—K2
Resigns.

GAME 41

STOLTZ–COLLE

Bled tournament, 1931.

ALEKHINE DEFENCE

1.	P—K4	Kt—KB3
2.	P—K5	Kt—Q4
3.	P—QB4	Kt—Kt3
4.	P—B5	Kt—Q4
5.	Kt—QB3	Kt×Kt
6.	QP×Kt	Kt—B3

The normal lines against the Lasker treatment of the Alekhine Defence are 6 . . . , P—Q3 or 6 . . . , P—K3. Black's irregular attempt to use the advanced White pawn as a target recoils horribly upon him.

7.	Kt—B3	P—KKt3
8.	B—QB4	B—Kt2

By his previous move Black has virtually committed himself to P—Q3 rather than P—K3, yet after White's reply he will be unable to play P—Q3 without losing a pawn. Should he attempt to overcome this by playing P—Q3 at once, then 9 Kt—Kt5 is a very strong reply. In fact, his 6th and 7th moves already stand condemned.

9.	B—B4	O—O
10.	Q—Q2	P—Kt3

Now the only possible development for the bishop, but Black is not allowed time to play B—Kt2.

11.	P—KR4	P—KR4

He is already in trouble, for he is faced with a series of White moves such as P—R5, P×P, B—KR6, B×B and Q—R6ch. But the text move only creates a new target for White to attack.

12.	O—O—O	P—K3

A sad necessity, but he is threatened with 13 Q—B2, K—R1 (against Q×P) ; 14 P—K6.

13.	B—KKt5	P—B3

Now his KKtP will be gravely weakened, but if Q—K1 ; 14 B—B6, and Black can hardly play B×B ; 15 P×B, K—R2 (against Q—R6) ; 16 B—Q3, threatening Q—Kt5 and Q×RPch.

14.	KP×P	B×P
15.	Q—B2	Q—K1

The only defence against the two threats of Q×Pch. and B×Pch.

16.	B—Q3	K—Kt2
17.	P—KKt4	RP×P
18.	QR—Kt1	

White prosecutes the attack vigorously. If now 18 . . ., P×Kt ; 19 B×P, Q—K2 (Q×B ; 20 B×Bch.) ; 20 B—R5, K—R1 (R—R1 ; 21 Q—Kt6ch., or B×Bch. ; 21 P×B, Kt—K4 ; 22 Q—K4) ; 21 Q—Kt6, Kt—K4 (Q—Kt2 ; 22 B×B) ; 22 Q—R6ch., Q—R2 ; 23 Q×Rch.

18.		B×Bch.
19.	Kt×B	Kt—K4
20.	B—K4	B—R3

In his almost hopeless position Black must go all out or go under, so having temporarily stopped the K side attack, he offers a sacrifice of the exchange.

21. B×R

White's attack has brought him a gain of material, but he would be better advised not to take it, for it means abandoning all pressure on Black. Better was the further prosecution of the attack by some such line as 21 P—R5, P×P; 22 P—B3, R—QKt1; 23 KBP×P, Kt×P; 24 R×Kt, P×R; 25 R—R7ch., K—B3 (K—Kt1; 26 Q—R2); 26 Q—B2ch., and mates next move.

21. Kt—Q6ch.
22. K—Kt1 Q×B

Not R×P; 23 Q—R4, Kt×BP; 24 Q—Q4ch.

23. P—QB4 Kt—K4
24. Q—B3 R—B4
[Diagram 53]

25. P—B4

He wants to play R—K1, which at the moment is no threat because R×Kt would be answered by Q×Rch., so he evolves a problem-like manœuvre to induce Black to block the diagonal himself. But unfortunately it is not quite sound and Black is given a strong passed pawn. Better was the slower line 25 R—K1, P×P; 26 KR—Kt1, P—Q3; 27 Kt×Pch., K—Kt1; 28 R×P.

(BLACK) COLLE

(WHITE) STOLTZ

Position before White's 25th move.

(DIAGRAM 53)

25. P×P e.p.
26. R—K1 P—B7
27. R×Kt

The first point of the combination as White saw it. If now Q×Rch.; 28 R—K1 dis. ch., wins.

27. K—Kt1
28. R—KB1 Q—Kt7
29. Q—Q3

The second point of the combination as White saw it. The threat against both rooks is met, for if now R×R; 30 Q×Pch., and mates.

29. B×P

The real point of the combination, seen by Black, and a beautiful one.

30. Q×B R×R
31. Q—Q3 Q×Rch.

A splendid climax, leading to

32 Q×Q, R—Q8ch. The threat of 31 . . ., Q×Rch. ; could not be avoided, for if 31 K—B2, then R×P.

[Resigns.

An object lesson in refusing to reconcile oneself to impending resignation, however hopeless the situation may appear. A game is never lost until it is won.

F. D. Yates (1884–1932) was many times British champion and a frequent competitor in International tournaments. His style displayed great tenacity and determination, and though he was not sufficiently consistent to win the highest prizes, there were few masters whom he did not beat in his time.

GAME 42

EUWE–YATES

Hastings tournament, 1932.

KING'S INDIAN DEFENCE

1.	P—Q4	Kt—KB3
2.	P—QB4	P—KKt3
3.	Kt—QB3	B—Kt2
4.	P—K4	P—Q3
5.	P—B3	

The most combinative line against the King's Indian Defence, preparing O—O—O, followed by P—KKt4 and P—KR4.

5.		O—O
6.	B—K3	Kt—B3
7.	KKt—K2	P—K4
8.	Q—Q2	Kt—Q2
9.	O—O—O	

More in keeping with the usual forms of the opening would be 9 P—Q5, Kt—K2 ; 10 P—KKt4, followed by 11 Kt—Kt3. Now Black has succeeded in forcing P—KB4 if he wishes, but he unwisely tries first to force the White KKt in front of the KKtP.

9.		Kt—Kt3
10.	P—QKt3	

Giving Black a point of attack, but he has calculated that it is immune for the time being at least.

10.		P—QR4

If White had played the usual P—Q5, this would be correct, but now his centre is completely destroyed. White's reply threatens B×Kt.

11	P×P	P—R5

It is neck or nothing, so he sacrifices a piece for an attack 11 . . ., P×P would be answered by 12 Q×Q, R×Q; 13 R×Rch., Kt×R; 14 B×Kt, P×B; 15 Kt—Q5, winning.

12.	B×Kt	RP×P
13.	B—K3	

Stronger was RP×P and Black could hardly risk 13 . . ., P×B; but would have to try 13 . . ., B×P; 14 B—K3, Kt—R4; 15 Q—B2, with variations similar to the actual game but with White a QKtP to the good. The loss of this pawn makes itself felt later.

13.		P×RP
14.	Kt×P	B×P
15.	KKt—B3	B—K3
16.	P—B4	Kt—R4
17.	Q—B2	B—Kt2
18.	Kt—Q5	P—QB3
19.	B—Kt6	Q—Kt1
20.	Kt—B7	P—Q4

A fighting continuation, for he may as well be hung for a sheep as a lamb. To be a major instead of a minor piece down is of small importance in such a position. White could safely reply 21 Kt×R, Q×Pch.; 22 K—Kt1, R×Kt; 23 B—Q4, but not 23 B×Kt, R×B; 24 B—Q3, Q—K4. The Black rook, however, cannot escape, and he prefers to close the long diagonal first.

21.	P—K5	B—B4

(BLACK) YATES

(WHITE) EUWE

Position before White's 22nd move.

(DIAGRAM 54)

22.	B—Q3	

This likely looking move gives Black a fighting chance. Better was Q—R4, Kt×P; 23 Q×R (not Kt×R, Q×P; 24 P×Q, B—R3ch.; 25 R—Q2, B×Rch.; 26 K—Q1, Kt—Kt 7ch.; 27 K×B, Kt×Q; with good chances), Kt×B; 24 Q×Q, R×Q; and White has reduced Black's chances of complicating almost to nothing.

22.		B×B
23.	R×B	Kt×P
24.	Kt×R	Q×Kt
25.	B—Q4	R—B1

Playing for a rapid advance of his three united passed pawns, the only line that offers any real hope.

26.	R—K1	

Not P—K6 because of B×B; 27 P×Pch., K×P; 28 R×

B, Q—R6ch.; 29 K—Kt1, Q—B4; threatening Kt—R6ch.

26. P—QB4
27. B—R1 P—QKt4
28. R—K2 P—Kt5
29. Q—Kt3

If 29 Q—Q1, P—Kt6; but unlikely as it seems the move selected allows Black to achieve virtual equality, and R—QKt3 was better.

29. Kt×P

A brilliant knight manœuvre. If 30 P×Kt, P—B5.

30. R×P P—B5
31. Q—KR3

The only way to defend his rook is to counter-attack Black's rook, but the move leaves him open to a multiple fork.

31. Kt—Q6ch.
32. K—Kt1 Kt×P

The culmination of his knight manœuvres. At first sight he seems to recover a whole rook with a won ending, but White discovers an ingenious move to remain a minor piece ahead.

33. R—QR5 Kt×Q

Now it is Black's turn to fail to take full advantage of the position. He should play Q—B3; 34 Q—K3 (not Kt×P, R—QKt1), Kt×R; 35 B×B, K×B; 36 Q×Kt, keeping two pieces, one to defend the pawns and one to attack on the other flank. Now his Q side pawns will fall.

34. R×Q R×R
35. B×B K×B
36. P×Kt P—Kt6
37. Kt—B3 R—Q1
38. K—Kt2 R—Q6
39. Kt—R4 R×P

His only chance now lies on the K side.

40. Kt—Kt6 P—Kt4
41. Kt×P P—B4
42. Kt—Q2 K—B3
43. Kt×P P—R4
44. K—B2 P—B5
45. Kt—Q4 P—R5
46. K—Q2 R—R6
47. K—K1 P—R6
48. R—K6ch K—B2
49. R—K5 K—Kt3
50. Kt—K2

All the White pieces have got across to the defence just in time and the game is a legitimate draw.

50. R—R7
51. K—B2 K—B3
52. R—B5 P—Kt5
53. R—B4 P—B6
54. R×P P×Kt
55. R—KR4 Drawn.

M. Sultan Khan (b. 1905) came to Europe in 1929, and left again four years later as suddenly as he had arrived. In that time he had shown himself, for all his lack of book knowledge and inability to read any textbook, one of the world's great masters, winning many prizes in tournaments, winning the British championship and defeating Tartakower in a match.

GAME 43

SULTAN KHAN–ALEKHINE

Folkestone team tournament, 1933.
(Great Britain—France)

QUEEN'S PAWN GAME

1. Kt—KB3 P—Q4
2. P—Q4 P—QB4
3. P—B3 Kt—QB3
4. P—KKt3 Kt—B3
5. B—Kt2 P—K3
6. O—O B—Q3
7. QKt—Q2

White is playing the Grunfeld Defence with a move in hand and the colours reversed; as a result he gets less than he should from the advantage of the first move.

7. P×P
8. P×P O—O
9. P—Kt3

Initiating a long struggle for control of the centre; his plan is to control his K5 and then if possible follow with P—K4.

9. B—Q2
10. B—Kt2 Q—Kt1

Countering White's pressure on his K4 and at the same time preparing the advance of his Q side pawns.

11. R—K1 R—Q1

Preparing an action against the QP should White play P—K4.

12. Q—Kt1 P—KR3
13. P—QR3 P—QR4
14. B—KB1 Kt—K2
15. P—K3 B—B3
16. B—Q3 Kt—Q2
17. B—B3 P—QKt4
18. B—Kt2

A better way of meeting the threat of P—Kt5, opening a file, was P—QR4, P—Kt5; 19 B—Kt2. As played his QB4 is weakened.

18. P—R5
19. P—QKt4 Kt—QKt3
20. B—B3 Kt—B5
21. R—R2 P—B4
22. Q—R1

P—K4 being now prevented, he makes every effort to play Kt—K5.

22. Kt—KKt3
23. B—B1 Q—B2
24. R—B1 QR—B1

25. R(2)—B2 Q—Kt1
26. B—KKt2 R—B1
27. Kt—K1 Kt—R1
28. Kt×Kt

He wants to play P—B4 so as to win the battle for his K5, but can only do it by allowing Black a passed QBP.

28. KtP×Kt
29. P—B4 Kt—B2
30. Kt—B3 B—K2

Beginning a new counter-action against his K4 by threatening P—Kt4.

31. Kt—K5 Kt—Q3
32. B—B3

After his efforts to establish his knight he does not want to exchange it for Black's KB, so there is no point in 32 Kt—Kt6, R—KB2; 33 B—B3, B—B3; followed by 34 . . ., K—R2. Instead he prepares for the impending action on the KKt file.

32. K—R2
33. R—KKt2 P—Kt4
34. Q—Kt1 Kt—K5
35. Q—B2 R—Kt1

An inaccuracy which should have cost him the initiative as well as a pawn. Better was B—Kt4.

36. B×Kt BP×B
37. Kt×B R×Kt
38. Q×P R—B2
39. R—R1

Missing his chance, as Black's 40th move now holds up the pawns indefinitely. Correct was 39 Q—B2, R—R2; 40 P—QR4, threatening 41 R—Kt1, for if 40 . . ., B×P; 41 R—Kt1, R—QKt2; 42 Q—Kt2, and wins. Now Black reassumes the initiative in this delicately balanced game.

39. R—R2
40. Q—Q1 Q—KB1
41. R—KB2 P×P
42. R×P Q—Kt2
43. R—B2

Not P—QR4, B—Kt4.

43. B—Q3
44. R(1)—R2

And now if P—QR4, then B×KKtP; 45 P×B, Q×Pch.; 46 K—B1, Q×P; 47 Q—Q2 (Q—K1, Q—R6ch.; 48 K—K2, Q—Q6 Mate. Or 47 B—Kt2, R(2)—KKt2), Q—R6ch.; 48 K—K2, R—Kt6; 49 B—Kt2, P—K6; 50 Q—B2ch., K—Kt1; threatening R—Kt7ch., when the White rook moves.

44. Q—Kt4
45. Q—QB1 R(2)—KKt2
46. R—KKt2

Now the threat of P—R4—R5 by Black prevents a Q side advance.

46. P—R4
47. B—K1 P—R5

[Diagram 55]

48. K—R1

If 48 P×P, Q×Rch.; 49 R×Q, R×Rch.; 50 K—B1, R—Kt8ch.; 51 K—K2, R(1)—Kt7ch.; 52 K—Q1, B×RP; threatening B—Kt6, winning.

48. Q—Kt5
49. R(R)—KB2 P×P

(BLACK) ALEKHINE

(WHITE) SULTAN KHAN

Position before White's 48th move.

(DIAGRAM 55)

Missing the decisive line. Kashdan pointed out that the correct move was 49 . . ., Q—R 6; threatening P×P, and if 50 P—Kt4, R×P; 51 R×R (Q—Q2, Q×Pch.; 52 R×Q, R—Kt8 Mate), R×R; 52 B—B3, B×RP; wins. Now Black will have great difficulty in winning.

50. P×P B×KKtP
51. R×B

Not 51 R—R2ch., B×R; 52 R×Bch., K—Kt3; 53 R—KKt2, K—B4; 54 R×Q, R×R; and mate cannot be avoided.

51. Q×R
52. R—R2ch. Q×Rch.
53. K×Q R—Kt7ch.
54. K—R3 R—Kt8

Winning the bishop by the threat of R—R8 Mate.

55. K—R2 R(1)—Kt7ch.
56. K—R3 R—K7
57. Q—Q1

The only move to save the queen against the threat of R(8) ×B, followed by R×Pch.

57. R(8)×B
58. Q—R4 R×Pch.
59. K—Kt2 R(6)—K7ch.
60. K—Kt3 R—Kt8ch.
61. K—B4 R—B7ch.
62. K—K5 R—Kt3

Black has a potential win with his passed pawns, but he will have difficulty in avoiding perpetual check. The struggle between Black's winning chances and White's drawing chances is one of absorbing interest and intensity.

63. Q—Q7ch. K—R3
64. Q—Q8 P—K6

Q—R4ch., was threatened.

65. Q—R8ch. K—Kt4
66. Q—R3 R—B4ch.
67. K—Q6 K—B5
68. Q—B1ch.

White succeeds in getting rid of the dangerous Black KP, but at the cost of his own QP.

68. K—K5
69. Q—Kt1ch.

Not Q—Q1, P—K4 dis. ch.; 70 K—K7, P×P.

69. K×P
70. Q—Q1ch. K—B6

An amazing conception. He could escape perpetual check with 70 . . ., K—K5; continuing as he does on the 76th move, but first he plans to allow a temporary series of checks merely in order to win White's RP.

71. Q—B1ch. K—Kt6
72. Q—Kt1ch. K×P
73. Q—R1ch. K—Kt6

The key to the Black king's outing; he does not seek to win the KtP as well, for after 73 . . ., K×P; 74 Q—Kt2ch., K—R4; 75 Q—R3ch., K—Kt3; 76 Q—B5ch., with an easy perpetual check.

74. Q—Kt1ch. K—B6
75. Q—R1ch. K—Q6
76. Q—Q1ch. K—K5
77. Q—Kt1ch. K—B5
78. Q—B1ch. K—Kt4
79. Q—Kt1ch. K—R3
80. Q×Pch. R(B)—Kt4
81. Q—QB3

Threatening Q—R8 Mate. The checks are temporarily over, for after 81 Q—R3ch., K—Kt2; 82 Q—B3ch., K—Kt1; 83 Q—QR3, R—Kt6; 84 Q—R8ch., K—Kt2; 85 Q—Kt 7ch., K—R3; White is right out of position for making any progress towards his draw.

81. K—R2
82. K—B6

The delicacy of the position is shown by the fact that if White tries 82 P—Kt5, P—Q5; 83 Q×BP (of course not Q×QP, R—Q4ch.), R—Q4ch.; 84 K—B7 (or K—K7, P—Q6; 85 Q—R4ch., K—Kt2; 86 Q—K1, P—Q7; 87 Q—Q1, P—K4; winning), P—Q6; 85 Q—R4 ch., K—Kt1; 86 Q—K4, K—Kt2; 87 Q—KR4, P—Q7; 88 Q—K7ch., K—Kt1; 89 Q—K8ch., K—R2; 90 Q—K7ch., R—Kt2.

82. R—Kt6
83. Q—B1 P—B6
84. P—Kt5 P—Q5
85. P—Kt6 R—Kt8
86. Q—B2 R(8)—Kt7
87. Q—B1 R—Kt7
88. P—Kt7 P—K4 dis. ch.

(BLACK) ALEKHINE

(WHITE) SULTAN KHAN

Position before White's 89th move.

(DIAGRAM 56)

89. K—B5

A bold and clever attempt to keep drawing chances by bringing the king to counter the Black pawns, his own pawn remaining immune because of the threat of Q—R1ch. Worse than useless would be 89 K—B7, R—Kt2ch.; and the pawn is lost.

89. R(3)—Kt3
90. Q—B1

Another fighting move, for if 90 . . ., R×P; 91 Q—B5ch., and the Black pawns fall if Black tries to avoid perpetual check.

90. K—Kt2
91. Q—B5 R(7)—Kt4ch.
92. K—B4 P—B7

It is Black's turn to play a bold and ingenious move with a pawn. After 92 . . ., R×P; Black might just escape perpetual check, but the text is more decisive. The pawn is immune because of the very unusual and attractive line 93 Q×BP, R—B3ch.; 94 K×R, R×Q; 95 P—Kt8=Q, R—Kt7ch.; winning the second queen in the same way as the first.

93. Q—Kt5ch. K—B2

Perpetual check is just avoidable, but in the most surprising way, for the key square is K6, to reach which the Black king has somehow to get to the other side of the White queen, at first sight an impossible feat.

94. Q—B5ch. K—K2
95. Q—Kt5ch. K—Q2
96. Q—B5ch. K—B2
97. Q—B8ch.

The alternative 97 Q—B7ch., K—Kt1; 98 Q—B8ch., K×P; 99 Q—K7ch., K—R3; 100 Q—R3ch., R—R4; leads nowhere. Thus the Black king has succeeded in getting round the White queen.

97. K—Q3
98. Q—Q8ch. K—K3
99. Q—B8ch. K—B3
100. K—Q3

To drive the king further would only assist Black's game. For example, 100 Q—B8ch., K—Kt4; 101 Q—K7ch., K—B5; 102 Q—R4ch., K—K6; 103 Q—Kt5ch., K—K7; 104 Q—Kt2ch., K—Q8; 105 Q—B1 ch., K—Q7; 106 Q—B2ch., K—B8; 107 Q—K1ch., K—Kt7.

100. R×P
101. Q—R8ch.

If Q×P, R—Kt6ch.; 102 K—K4 (K—B4, R—B6ch.; or K—Q2, R—Kt7), R—K6ch.; 103 K—Q5, R—Q2ch.; and 104 . . ., R—B6ch.; winning easily.

101. K—Kt4
102. K×P

There is still no perpetual check, for if 102 Q—Kt8ch., K—B5; 103 Q—B8ch., K—Kt6; 104 Q—Kt8ch., K—B7; 105 Q—B8ch., K—K8; and the checks are over with Black in an improved position, for if now 106 K×P, P—K5; threatening an unavoidable mate in two.

102 R—Q2
103. Q—Kt8ch. K—B5
104. Q—B8ch. K—K5
105. Q—R8ch. R(2)—Kt2
106. K—Q2

A queen move, unpinning the rook would allow 106 . . ., R—Kt7ch.; 107 K—Q1, R—Kt

8ch.; 108 K—K2, R(2)—Kt7 Mate. The tremendous struggle is over at last.

106. R—Kt7ch.
107. K—K1 K—K6
108. K—B1

Of course if 108 Q—R3ch, R(2)—Kt6; with mate to follow, but mate follows the text move also.

108. R—B7ch.
Resigns.

GAME 44

SPIELMANN–LASKER

Moscow tournament, 1935.

SCOTCH GAME

1. P—K4 P—K4
2. Kt—KB3 Kt—QB3
3. P—Q4 P×P
4. Kt×P Kt—B3
5. Kt—QB3 B—Kt5
6. Kt×Kt KtP×Kt
7. B—Q3 P—Q4
8. P×P Q—K2ch.

The usual P×P is better, but Lasker as so often seeks to bring about a difficult game in the hope of out-manœuvring his opponent.

9. Q—K2 Q×Qch.
10. K×Q P×P
11. Kt—Kt5 K—Q1
12. R—Q1 P—B3
13. P—QB3 R—K1ch.

If P×Kt; 14 P×B, P—QR3; 15 B—Kt5, threatening B—B2 and B—Kt3.

14. K—B1 B—B1
15. Kt—Q4 K—B2
16. B—B4ch. K—Kt3

Here B—Q3; 17 B×Bch., K×B; 18 Kt—B5ch., B×Kt; 19 B×B, would bring about the draw which Black is trying to avoid.

17. P—QR4 P—QR4
18. P—QKt4

With the better game, White feels in a position to start an attack. This sacrifice of a pawn and the resulting passed RP create considerable difficulties for Black.

18. P×P
19. P—R5ch. K—Kt2

The loss of the exchange by B—B7ch. would be enough to deter Black from R×P, though actually he would run into mate by 20 R×R, K×R; 21 B—B7ch., K—R5; 22 R—R1 Mate.

20. P×P Kt—K5

If B×P; 21 KR—Kt1, P—B4; 22 Kt—B2, with much the better game. The RP is now a formidable threat.

[Diagram 57]

21. Kt×P P—Kt4

Black has got more than he bargained for. He cannot meet White's pretty attack by K×Kt because of 22 QR—B1ch.,

(BLACK) LASKER

(WHITE) SPIELMANN

Position before White's 21st move.

(DIAGRAM 57)

K—Q2 (K—Kt2; 23 R—B7ch., K—Kt1; 24 R—K7 dis. ch.); 23 B—Kt5ch., K—K2 (K—Q1; 24 R×Pch.); 24 R—B 7ch., B—Q2; 25 R×P, KR—Q1; 26 B×B (threatening both B—B5 dis. ch. and R—K5ch.), R×B (Kt—B3; 27 B—Q6 Mate); 27 R(5)×Rch., winning easily. Or if 25 . . ., KR—B1; 26 R(5)×Bch., K—K3; 27 B—B4ch., K—B4; 28 R×Pch., K—Kt3; 29 B—Q3, R×R; 30 R×R, R—K1; 31 P—B3, winning. Black therefore gives up the KKtP in order to force the White QB off its diagonal and by the threat of K×Kt to win the White QKtP.

22.	B×Kt	R×B
23.	Kt—Q8ch.	K—R3
24.	B×P	B—K3

He cannot take the KtP yet because of Kt×P, remaining two pawns ahead.

25. Kt—B6

After Kt×B, P×Kt; 26 B—Q2, B×P; 27 B×B, R×B; White would lose the QRP and Black would draw.

25. B—Kt2

He finds he still cannot play B×P because of 26 QR—Kt1, after which the bishop cannot move because of R—Kt6 Mate, for if B—QB4; 27 B—K7, is decisive and if B×P; 27 Kt×B, K×Kt; 28 R—R1ch., R—R5; 29 R×Rch., K×R 30 R—R1ch. The only reply would be 26 . . ., K—Kt4; and then follows 27 Kt—Q4ch., K—B5 (K—B4; 28 B—K7ch., or K—R5; 28 R—R1ch., B—R6; 29 B—B1); 28 QR—B1ch., B—B6; 29 Kt—K2, P—Q5; 30 P—B3, R—K4; 31 R×Pch., and wins.

26.	QR—B1	R—QB5
27.	B—K3	K—Kt4

Forced, to prevent White consolidating with B—B5.

28.	Kt—R7ch.	K×P
29.	B—Kt6	

Black has successfully survived the first phase. The struggle now shifts to the QRP.

29.		R—B6
30.	R—Kt1ch.	R—Kt6
31.	Kt—B6ch.	K—R5
32.	B—Q4	

Unless he can get a rook on to the QR file he can never advance the pawn.

32. R×R
33. R×R B×B
34. Kt×B R—R3

The pawn is still taboo, for if K×P; 35 R—R1ch., and if R×P; 35 R—R1ch., K—Kt5; 36 Kt—B6ch., winning the rook either way.

35. R—R1ch. K—Kt5
36. K—K2 B—Q2
37. Kt—B2ch.

If K—Q2, B—R5; and the RP falls.

37. K—B6
38. Kt—K3 B—Kt4ch.
39. K—K1

K—Q1 is no better because of P—Q5; 40 Kt—Q5ch., K—Kt7; 41 R—B1, B—K7ch.; 42 K—Q2, R×P.

39. P—Q5
40. R—B1ch.

Now if Kt—Q5ch., K—Kt7; 41 R—Q1, R—K3ch.; 42 K—Q2, R—K7 Mate. White, so far from having a win, suddenly finds he must take care to avoid a loss.

40. K—Q6

Black is also not out of danger, for if K—Kt7; 41 R—B5, P×Kt (not R×P; 42 Kt—B4ch.); 42 R×Bch., K—B6; 43 P×P, with still some definite winning chances.

41. R—Q1ch.

If R—B5, B—R5; 42 Kt—B5, R—K3ch.; 43 K—B1, K—Q7; 44 P—Kt3, B—B3.

Drawn.

A game that was in the balance up to the very last move.

GAME 45

EUWE–ALEKHINE

19th match game, Eindhoven, 1937.

NIMZO-INDIAN DEFENCE

1. P—Q4 Kt—KB3
2. P—QB4 P—K3
3. Kt—QB3 B—Kt5
4. Kt—B3 Kt—K5

Premature. The knight will have to return shortly.

5. Q—B2 P—Q4
6. P—K3 P—QB4
7. B—Q3 Kt—KB3

For if Kt×Kt, he will have the utmost difficulty in castling.

8. BP×P KP×P
9. P×P B×P

Black's lack of development still hampers his castling. For example if now O—O; 10 O—O, B×P; 11 P—K4, P×P (P—Q5; 12 Kt—K2, B—Kt3; 13 B—KKt5, wins); 12 Kt×P, B—K2; 13 Kt×Ktch, winning a pawn. Or if 11 . . ., Kt×P; 12 Kt×P, Kt×P; 13

B×Pch., K—R1; 14 Q×B, wins.

10. O—O Kt—B3
11. P—K4 B—K2

If Kt—QKt5; 12 B—Kt5ch., B—Q2; 13 Q—K2, or if P×P; 12 Kt×P, Kt×Kt; 13 B×Kt, with advantage.

12. P—K5

In view of Black's difficulties he could afford to wait and secure himself with P—QR3.

12. Kt—KKt5
13. R—K1

B—KB4 was the winning line. Black now takes advantage of the vulnerability first of KB7 and then of QB7 to fight back. White will succeed in forcing Black to give up any idea of castling, but will now have to waste time with awkward defensive tactics.

13. Kt—Kt5
14. B—Kt5ch. K—B1

If B—Q2; 15 Q—B5, P—KR4; 16 P—K6, winning.

15. Q—K2 B—QB4
16. Kt—Q1 B—B4
17. P—KR3

[Diagram 58]

17. P—KR4

If Kt—B7, White gets two minor pieces for the rook, which is more than good value when Black's KR is shut in. Only by the most bold and imaginative play can Black still hope to save the game.

(BLACK) ALEKHINE

(WHITE) EUWE

Position before Black's 17th move.

(DIAGRAM 58)

18. B—Kt5

Now if P×Kt, P×P.; 19 Kt—Kt5 (forced, to prevent Q—R5), Kt—B7; 20 B—KB4 (to allow Kt—K3), P—Kt6. White could not play 20 Kt—K3, at once because of Q×Kt.

18. Q—Kt3
19. Kt—R4

And again if P×Kt, P×P; 20 Kt—R4, Black has the choice of Kt—B7 threatening Kt—Q5, or of P—Kt6.

19. B—K5
20. P×Kt Kt—B7
21. Kt—QB3 Kt—Q5
22. Q—B1 P×P
23. Kt—R4

Black has built up a threatening position at the cost of a piece. P—Kt6 has always to be guarded against, and White therefore tries to break up

Black's hold on the dangerous diagonal. Clearly if 23 Kt×B, then P×Kt; 24 B—K2, P—Kt6.

23.		Q—B2
24.	R×B	

The logical move was Kt×B, Q×Kt; 25 B—Q3, remaining a piece ahead, for if then R—R4; 26 QR—B1, Q—Kt3; 27 B—K3, R×Kt; 28 B×B, P×B; 29 KR—Q1, R—Q1; 30 Q—B4, wins. The speculative text move does not turn out so well.

24.		P×R
25.	Q—B4	R—B1
26.	R—B1	P—QKt3
27.	Kt×B	P×Kt
28.	B—QR6	

Subsequent events show that P—K6 was better with the probable continuation Kt×P; 29 Kt—Kt6ch., P×Kt; 30 Q×Kt. As played, Black will surprisingly recover all his lost material.

28.		Q×P
29.	B×R	Q×B
30.	Q×QBPch.	

For if now P—KKt3, then R×Kt; 31 P×R, Q×Rch.; 32 Q×Q, Kt—K7ch.; with at least an equal ending.

30.		Q×Q
31.	R×Q	R×Kt
32.	R—B4	Kt—K7ch.
33.	K—B1	Kt—B5
34.	K—Kt1	P—Kt6
35.	B—R6	

Of course if R×P, Kt—R6ch.; wins the rook, and if P×P, Kt—K7ch.; 36 K—B1, Kt×Pch. Black comes out a pawn ahead and actually tries to win, but there proves to be not quite enough in it. A most astonishing recovery.

35.		P×Pch.
36.	K×P	R—R3
37.	R×P	R×B
38.	R×Kt	R×P
39.	R—QKt4	P—Kt3
40.	R—Kt7	K—Kt2
41.	K—B3	P—Kt4
42.	P—QKt4	K—Kt3
43.	P—Kt5	P—B4
44.	P—Kt6	R—R6ch.
45.	K—B2	P—R3
46.	R—Kt8	R—QKt6
47.	P—Kt7	K—Kt2
48.	R—QR8	R×P
49.	R×P	Drawn.

M. Botvinnik (b. 1911) began to win his great reputation in 1932, when he carried off the Russian championship. In a nation of many masters he has consistently shown himself the greatest. His tournament successes include Leningrad, 1934, Moscow, 1935, Nottingham, 1936, and Groningen, 1946.

S. Reshevsky (b. 1911) was taken as a child prodigy to America and became a United States citizen. He reappeared in the 1930's as a fully fledged master, and rapidly proved himself the strongest player in America. His tournament successes include the sharing of 1st prize in the strong tournament at Kemeri, 1937.

GAME 46

RESHEVSKY–BOTVINNIK

Avro tournament, 1938.

NIMZO-INDIAN DEFENCE

1. P—Q4 Kt—KB3
2. P—QB4 P—K3
3. Kt—QB3 B—Kt5
4. P—K3 O—O
5. Kt—K2 P—Q4
6. P—QR3 B—K2
7. P×P Kt×P
8. Kt×Kt P×Kt
9. P—KKt3

Deciding that the pressure of his bishop on the centre is worth the weakness of the White squares.

9. Kt—Q2
10. B—Kt2 Kt—B3
11. O—O B—Q3
12. Kt—B3 P—B3
13. P—QKt4 P—QR3
14. R—K1 R—K1
15. B—Kt2 B—B1
16. Q—Q3 B—K3
17. P—B3 Kt—Q2
18. Kt—R4 P—QKt3

The apparent weakness of the QBP after this move will be effectively covered from attack by the movement of the Black knight to QB5. There is no real reason for not playing the pawn to the 4th at once.

19. QR—B1 P—QKt4
20. Kt—B5 Kt—Kt3
21. B—B3 R—R2
22. P—K4 Kt—B5
23. R—R1 B×Kt

So far the game has been one of careful and slow development. Now Black prepares to invade White's game along the Q file.

24. QP×B R—Q2
25. Q—Q4 P—B3
26. P—B4 P×P
27. Q×KP R—Q6
28. QR—B1 R×B

This sacrifice, based on the resulting weakness of White's KR, turns out a somewhat doubtful speculation.

29. R×R B—B2
30. R—Q3

Not Q—Kt1 because of Q—Q5ch., winning. White fights every move from this point.

30. Q—Kt1
31. R(K)—Q1 R×Q
32. B×R

Of course if R—Q8ch., R—K1; and Black wins a piece.

32. Q—KB1
33. R—Q8 B—K1
34. R—K1

Most ingenious. The more obvious B×BP would be answered by B×B; 35 R×Q ch., K×R; with good chances for Black. Now Black cannot prevent White recovering the piece and coming out with two rooks for the queen.

34. K—B2
35. B×RP
[Diagram 59]

(BLACK) BOTVINNIK

(WHITE) RESHEVSKY

Position before Black's 35th move.

(DIAGRAM 59)

35. Kt—K4

Another ingenuity, this time by Black, who hopes by this to keep the rooks split and to retain complications.

36. P×Kt Q—R1
37. B—B2 K—K2
38. R—B8

Black's plan succeeds, for White now makes a slip. The rook needs to go one square further, to Kt8, as will appear.

38. P—B4
39. B×P Q—R4
40. P—Kt4 Q—Kt4
41. R—B7ch.

With the rook on QKt8 White could now play R—Kt7ch., K—B1 (K—Q1; 42 R—Q1ch., winning); 42 B—R7, threatening R—B1ch., winning.

41. K—Q1
42. R—B8ch. K—K2
43. P—K6 P—Kt3
44. R—B7ch. K—Q1
45. R—Q7ch.

A last desperate attempt to win, based on the passed KP. If in reply B×R, then 46 P—K7ch., Q×P (not K—K1; 47 B×Bch., and the pawn queens); 47 R×Q, K×R; 48

B×B, K×B; 49 P—KR4, wins.

45. K—B1
46. P—K7 P×B
47. R—Q8ch. K—B2
48. R×B Q×Pch.
49. K—R1 Q—B6ch.
50. K—Kt1 Q—Kt5ch.

Drawn.

P. Keres (b. 1916) is the most brilliantly combinative player among all the young masters. His gifts are allied with deep positional judgment and he was thus able to take 1st prize in his first major International tournament, the great contest at Semmering, 1937, and to follow it up by winning the Avro tournament of 1938. He is an Estonian by birth.

GAME 47

EUWE–KERES

Avro tournament, 1938.

DUTCH DEFENCE

1. P—Q4 P—K3
2. P—QB4 B—Kt5ch.
3. Kt—B3 P—KB4
4. Q—Kt3 Q—K2
5. P—QR3

The orthodox P—KKt3 would be answered by 5 . . ., Kt—QB3; 6 Kt—B3, Kt—R4. Black's withholding of Kt—KB3 has gained him a move elsewhere with some effect. White must therefore take preliminary steps before he can play P—KKt3.

5. B×Ktch.
6. Q×B Kt—KB3
7. P—KKt3 P—Q3
8. Kt—B3

If B—Kt2, P—K4. The game now transposes into a kind of Queen's Indian Defence where Black has no need to play Kt—K5 in order to get in P—KB4.

8. P—QKt3
9. B—Kt2 B—Kt2
10. O—O QKt—Q2
11. P—QKt4 O—O
12. B—Kt2 QR—B1
13. KR—Q1 P—B4
14. QP×P KtP×P

He must accept the weakness of the centre pawns, for if QP×P; 15 Kt—K5, B×B; 16 K×B, KR—Q1; 17 P—Kt5, threatening Kt—B6.

15. Q—Q3 Kt—Kt3

Black has calculated accurately that his pawn position is defensible owing to this counter-attack. If now 16 Q×QP, then Q×Q; 17 R×Q, Kt×P; 18 B×Kt, Kt×R; 19 B—K7, Kt—K5; 20 B×R, K×B; with approximate equality.

16.	P—Kt5	KR—Q1
17.	P—QR4	P—Q4
18.	P×P	R×P
19.	Q—B2	R×Rch.
20.	Q×R	

He must defend his QRP. If 20 R×R, then B—K5; 21 Q—Kt3, P—QB5; 22 Q—R2, Q—Kt5.

20.		Kt—B5
21.	B—QB1	

Somewhat better was B×Kt, Q×B; 22 R—B1.

21.		P—K4

For now Black could play Kt—K5 with a very aggressive position. The text move seriously weakens the diagonal on to his king.

22.	Q—Kt3	B—Q4
23.	Kt—Q2	

The game becomes complicated. The bishop is attacked, and therefore indirectly the knight also. Less good was 23 Kt—R4, P—K5; 24 Kt×P, Q—K4.

23.		P—K5

After the alternative Kt—Kt3; 24 B×Bch., Kt(Kt)×B; 25 Kt—B4, the White Q side pawns are a danger.

24.	Kt×Kt	Q—K3
25.	B—R3	B×Kt
26.	Q—B2	B—Q4
27.	P—R5	

Naturally not 27 B×BP, Kt—Q2.

27.		B—Kt2
28.	B—Kt2	Kt—Q4
29.	Q—B4	P—R4
30.	P—K3	K—R2
31.	R—Q1	P—Kt3
32.	B—KB1	R—B2
33.	Q—Kt3	R—Q2
34.	B—B4	K—R3
35.	P—R4	

(BLACK) KERES

(WHITE) EUWE

Position before Black's 35th move.

(DIAGRAM 60)

A most critical position, especially for Black. White has maintained his pressure on the White diagonal and also controls the long Black diagonal. Since he can make no progress on the White diagonal, a switch to the Black one by 35 B—R1, preparing Q—Kt2, seems indicated. Black is then in difficulty as the following lines show: 35 . . ., Q—Kt1; 36 Q—Kt2, Q—Q1 (Q—K3; 37 Q—R8ch., R—R2; 38 B—Kt 7ch., K—Kt4; 39 P—R4ch., K—Kt5; 40 K—Kt2, threatening B—K2 mate. Or 36 . . ., R—R2; 37 B×Kt, B×B; 38 Q—K5, B—Kt6; 39 Q—B4ch., P—Kt4; 40 R—Q6ch.); 37 B×Kt, B×B; 38 R×B, R×R; 39 Q—Kt7ch., K—Kt4; 40 P—R4ch. However, Black can just hold the attack off for the moment by 35 . . ., B—R1; 36 Q—Kt2, R—R2.

35. P—B5

He must counter-attack or die.

36. KP×P

The best chance, as H. Golombek pointed out, was for White also to be aggressive and play 36 R×Kt, B×R; 37 Q—B3, Q—Kt1; 38 B×B, R×B; 39 KP×P, threatening the immediate advance of the Q side pawns.

36. P—K6

The point of Black's counterplay. The long White diagonal is to be opened to his bishop and the KKtP weakened and made an object of attack.

37. B×Kt P—K7

The counter-attack has a magnificent finale. If 38 B×Q, R×Rch.; 39 K—R2, R—R8 Mate.

38. R—K1 Q×B
39. Q×Q R×Q
40. P—B3

If R×P, again R—Q8ch., and mates.

40. R—Q8
41. K—B2 Drawn.

R. Fine (b. 1914), the American master, first made a reputation as a member of the American team at the Folkestone tournament, 1933. Since then he has consistently shown himself one of the world's masters, his best result being 1st prize at the Moscow, 1937, tournament. He is a great theoretician in all phases of the game.

GAME 48

FINE–KERES

Avro tournament, 1938.

RUY LOPEZ

1. P—K4 P—K4
2. Kt—KB3 Kt—QB3
3. B—Kt5 P—QR3

4.	B—R4	Kt—B3
5.	O—O	B—K2
6.	Q—K2	P—QKt4
7.	B—Kt3	P—Q3
8.	P—QR4	B—Kt5

The most vigorous reply to White's immediate threat of P×P and his ultimate threat of R—Q1 followed by operations on the Q file. The alternative R—QKt1 is followed by 9 P×P, P×P; 10 P—B3, B—Kt5; 11 R—Q1, O—O; 12 P—Q4, and White has achieved his ideal development.

9.	P—B3	O—O
10.	P×P	P×P
11.	R×R	Q×R
12.	Q×P	

Safer was P—Q3, but White plays to win by disturbing the balance of the game. He must now be prepared to face considerable pressure on his Q side down the open QKt file.

12.		Kt—R2

Of course he cannot recover the pawn at once, for if Kt×P; 13 B—Q5. Nor is the likely looking Kt—QR4 sufficient after 13 B—B2, Kt×P; 14 B×Kt, Q×B; 15 Q×Kt, Q×QKt; with a precarious game.

13.	Q—K2	Q×P
14.	Q×Q	Kt×Q
15.	P—Q4	

The result of Black's subtle 12th move is now apparent, for White must submit to the disruption of his K side unless he plays the awkward B—Q1. If 15 Kt×P, P×Kt; 16 P—B3, B—B4 ch.; 17 P—Q4, P×P; 18 P×Kt, P×P dis. ch.; winning.

15.		B×Kt
16.	P×B	Kt—Kt4
17.	K—Kt2	

Still eschewing safe drawing lines. After 17 B×Kt, B×B; 18 P×P, P×P; 19 R—K1, B—B5; 20 R—K2 (against R—Kt1), R—Q1; 21 Kt—R3, the bishops of opposite colours indicate a probably impending draw. He prefers to keep two bishops and accept a slightly inferior pawn position.

17.		R—Kt1
18.	B—QB4	P×P
19.	P×P	Kt—K3
20.	P—Q5	

The best way of defending the QP. Black would get a passed QP after 20 B×Kt, P×B; 21 R—K1, K—B2; 22 Kt—B3, Kt—B3; 23 P—Q5, P×P.

20.		Kt—B4
21.	Kt—B3	Kt—B1
22.	R—K1	K—B1
23.	R—K2	P—B4
24.	Kt—Kt5	

If White were content to draw, the strong position of the knight would justify leaving it undisturbed and preferring 24 B—K3. But White now envisages combinative play based on the weakness of Black's QB3

24.		Kt—Kt3
25.	P—Kt3	Kt×QP
26.	Kt—Q4	

The point. He is not interested in recovering the pawn by 26 Kt×QP, B×Kt; 27 B×Kt.

26. Kt—Kt5

Any other move with the knight fails to guard his vital QB3, and White then wins by 27 R×B, K×R; 28 Kt—B6ch.

27. B—Q2

(BLACK) KERES

(WHITE) FINE

Position before Black's 27th move.

(DIAGRAM 61)

Again threatening to plant the knight on QB6 after B×Kt.

27. P—Q4
28. B×Kt

Insufficient would be 28 Kt×P, P×B; 29 R×B (Kt×B, R—Kt1), P×P; or 28 R×B, P×B (not K×R; 29 B×Kt, R×B; 30 Kt—B6ch.); 29 R×BP, P×P; 30 R×Kt, P—Kt7; in either case leaving Black with irresistible Q side pawns.

28. R×B
29. Kt—B6

The culmination of White's combination. If Black replies R—Kt3, then 30 Kt×B, P×B; 31 P×P, with a good game. But Black has conducted his defence with great perspicacity and reveals that he too is playing for a win by giving up the exchange for strong passed pawns.

29. P×B
30. Kt×R P×P
31. Kt—Q5 Kt—Q6

The brilliant move on which Black has based his counter-play. If now 32 Kt×B (not R×B, P—Kt7), Kt—B5ch., 33 K—B1, Kt×R; 34 Kt—Q5, P—Kt7; wins.

32. R—Q2 P—Kt7
33. R—Q1 P—B4

Now there begins an intense struggle around the pawns. If at once 33 . . ., Kt—B8; 34 Kt—B3, B—B3; 35 Kt—Kt1, P—B4; 36 R—Q2, P—QB5; 37 R—B2.

34. K—B1 P—QB5
35. R—Kt1

Not K—K2, allowing the Black knight to go to QB8 with check. The vital square in the struggle is now QB2.

35. B—B4
36. K—K2 B×P

A magnificent move, coolly establishing a majority on the other wing. White's apparently convincing reply has been allowed for to a nicety.

37. Kt—K3

(BLACK) KERES

(WHITE) FINE

Position before Black's 37th move.

(DIAGRAM 62)

37. P—B6
38. Kt—B2

Not to be deflected from his fight against the pawns. If 38 K×Kt, B×Kt; 39 K×P, B—B8; revealing the purpose of his 36th move.

38. Kt—K8

Brilliantly continuing his fight to control White's QB2. If now 39 Kt×Kt, B×Kt; 40 K or R×B, P—B7; or 40 K—Q3, B—Q7.

39. Kt—R3 B—B4
40. K×Kt

The only move by which he can keep a piece defending his QB2.

40. B×Kt
41. K—Q1 B—Q3
42. K—B2 B×P
43. R—KR1

The king can hold the two pawns on the Q side as easily as one, so rather than waste a move capturing one of them, White regards it as timely to prevent Black obtaining too great a majority on the other wing.

43. B—K4
44. R×P K—B2
45. R—R1 P—Kt4
46. R—K1 K—B3
47. R—KKt1 K—Kt3
48. R—K1 B—B3
49. R—KKt1 P—Kt5

A fine move forcing the issue. He only needs one passed pawn on this wing.

50. P×P P—B5
51. P—Kt5

Fighting to the end. If now 51 . . ., B×P; 52 K×P, draws.

51. B—Q5
52. R—Q1 B—K6
53. K×P B—B8
54. R—Q6ch.

K—B2 fails because the rook cannot hold the king and pawn on the other flank. He therefore plays to hold the Q side with the rook and bring the king over to the K side, but the latter part of this plan cannot be fulfilled.

54.		K×P
55.	R—Kt6	P—B6
56.	K—Q3	K—B5
57.	R—Kt8	K—Kt6
	Resigns.	

For one of the pawns get home after 58 R—Kt8ch., K—B7; 59 R—Kt8, K—B8; 60 K—K4 (R—Kt7, P—B7; 61 R—Kt8, K—K8; 62 R—K8ch., K—Q8), P—B7; 61 K—B3, K—K8; 62 R—K8ch., K—Q8; 63 R—Q8ch., B—Q7.

C. H. O'D. Alexander (b. 1909) is a brilliant British master of Irish extraction who won the British championship in 1938. His best tournament result so far is the 1st prize at Hastings, 1947.

GAME 49

BOTVINNIK–ALEXANDER

Anglo-Russian radio match, 1946.

NIMZO-INDIAN DEFENCE

1.	P—Q4	Kt—KB3
2.	P—QB4	P—K3
3.	Kt—QB3	B—Kt5
4.	P—K3	P—Q4
5.	P—QR3	B×Ktch.
6.	P×B	P—B4
7.	P×QP	KP×P
8.	B—Q3	O—O
9.	Kt—K2	P—QKt3
10.	P—QR4	

A move which introduces a critical element into the game, for the position is too simple after 10 O—O, B—R3; 11 B×B, Kt×B; 12 Q—Q3, Q—B1; 13 B—Kt2, P×P; 14 BP×P, Kt—B2; as in a game Reshevsky—Fine, New York, 1941. The text move threatens the squares QB5 by B—R3 and at a suitable moment QKt6 by P—R5. The QRP is however weaker on the 4th than on the 3rd rank, a fact which Black later turns to good account.

10. B—R3

The key move of Black's system of defence, intended to clarify the position in the centre by hindering White's P—K4.

11. B×B

If B—R3 at once, then B×B; 12 Q×B, P—B5; 13 Q—B2, R—K1; with positions similar to the actual game but with Black's QKt on a better square.

11. Kt×B
12. B—R3

Preventing the rapid movement of the Black knight to QB2 and K3, by the threat to the QBP.

12. R—K1
13. Q—Q3 P—B5

The only alternative was Q—B1, after which P—R5 is playable. Black must therefore allow the easing of the tension in the centre, and now White's P—K4, if he can manage to play it, fits into the position beautifully from a strategic point of view.

14. Q—B2 Q—Q2

Beginning a far-sighted plan to take advantage of the weakness of the QRP, by bringing the QKt to QKt6. This plan takes four moves, and White just has time to get a counterattack started in the centre.

15. O—O Kt—Kt1
16. QR—K1 Kt—B3
17. Kt—Kt3

If Kt—B1, against Kt—Kt6, then Kt—QR4; 18 P—B3, Kt—Kt6; 19 Kt×Kt, Q×P; and Black still achieves his strategical object. E. Klein recommended Kt—K5 as the best answer to the text move.

17. Kt—QR4
18. P—B3 Kt—Kt6
19. P—K4 Q×P
20. Q—Kt2

The attempt to save a move by B—Q6 fails against Kt—B4. But the need to play this time-wasting move results in Black getting a powerful Q side attack started.

20. P—QR4
21. P—K5 P—QKt4
22. B—Q6

After 22 P×Kt, P—Kt5; 23 Kt—B5, P×B; Black's pawns are so far advanced as to be a danger. Botvinnik prefers a line which prevents so rapid an advance of the Black pawns.

22. R—K3
23. P×Kt

But now Kt—B5 was strong. Alexander gives 23 Kt—B5, QR—K1 (Kt—K1; 24 Kt—K7 ch., K—R1; 25 Kt×P, Kt ×B; 26 Kt—Kt6); 24 Kt—K7ch., R(3)×Kt; 25 B×R, R×B; 26 P×Kt, R×R; 27 R×R, P—Kt5; 28 Q—KB2, threatening Q—Kt3.

23. R×B
24. P×P P—Kt5
25. R—K5 R—K1

He cannot allow White to control the K file. If Kt×P; 26 P×Kt, P—B6; 27 Q—B1, R—QB1 (Q—B3; 28 Kt—B5, R—K3; 29 Kt—K7ch.); 28 Kt—B5, R—Q2; 29 Q—Kt5, threatening Kt—R6 Mate, and if P×P; 26 Q×P, Q—Kt5; 27 Q—K3, Q—Kt3; 28 Kt—B5, R—K3; 29 R—K1, QR—K1; 30 Q—Kt 5.

26. P—B4

Not R(B)—K1, R×R; 27 R×R, Kt×P; 28 P×Kt, Q—

Q8ch.; 29 K—B2, P—B6; 30 Q—K2, Q×Qch.; 31 R×Q (threatening R—K8ch. and Kt—B5ch.), R—K3; with advantage. White must keep a rook on his back rank for the time being.

26. Q—Q2

Defending the QP before moving the other rook. The Q side is now strong enough to await the clearing of the issues elsewhere.

27. Q—K2 R(3)—K3
28. P—B5 R×R
29. P×R P×P

He must submit to pressure on his king, for if K×P; 30 Q—Kt4ch., K—R1; 31 Kt—R5, R—KKt1; 32 Q×Rch., K×Q; 33 Kt—B6ch., K—B1; 34 Kt×Qch., K—K2; 35 Kt—Kt6. He therefore continues to develop his own threats on the Q side, but with 30 Kt—R5 white could obtain the better game.

30. P—B6
[Diagram 63]

(BLACK) ALEXANDER

(WHITE) BOTVINNIK

Position before Black's 30th move.

(DIAGRAM 63)

30. Q—R2ch.

A bad spot for the queen as will appear. With Kt—Q5 he might seriously embarrass White, the sort of threat resulting being 31 Q—K3, Q—Kt5; 32 Q×P, Q×Kt; 33 Q×Q, Kt—K7ch.; 34 K—B2, Kt×Q; 35 K×Kt, P—Q5; with advantage, while if 31 Q—R5, then P—B7; 32 Q—R4, Kt—Kt6; 33 Kt—B5 (threatening Kt—R6 Mate) Q×Kt; 34 R×Q, P—B8=Qch.; winning.

31. K—R1 Kt—Q5
32. Q—K3 R—R1

The unfortunate corollary of his 30th and 31st moves. Only thus can he unpin the knight, and at the same time guard against Kt—B5.

33. Q×P P—R5
34. Q×Kt

A devastating and beautiful continuation, which demolishes Black's game.

34. Q×Q
35. Kt—B5 P—R4

The only answer to the threats of Kt—K7 Mate and Kt—R6 Mate.

36. Kt×Q R—K1
37. Kt—B5 P—Q5
38. P—K6 Resigns.

For if R×P; 39 Kt—R6ch., K—R2; 40 P—Kt8=Qch., and if P×P; 39 Kt—R6ch., K—R2; 40 P—B7.

V. Smyslov (b. 1921) is one of the youngest generation of Russian masters and has already shown himself to be a potential candidate for the highest honours.

Katetov is a prominent Czech player.

GAME 50

SMYSLOV—KATETOV

Moscow—Prague match, 1946.

French Defence

1. P—K4 P—K3
2. P—Q4 P—Q4
3. Kt—QB3 Kt—KB3
4. B—Kt5 P×P
5. Kt×P B—K2
6. B×Kt B×B
7. P—QB3 Kt—Q2
8. P—KB4

The natural and more usual move is Kt—B3. Black at once prepares to counter in the centre by P—QB4.

8. B—K2
9. Q—B2 P—QB4
10. Kt—B3 Q—B2
11. P—KKt3

If Kt—K5, P—B3; 12 Kt—Q3, P—B5; and the KBP is lost.

11. P—QKt3
12. O—O—O

More in harmony with the fianchetto of the KB was O—O as soon as possible, but after 12 B—Kt2, B—Kt2; 13 O—O, P×P; 14 Kt×P, B—B4; White's position is not altogether comfortable. He therefore decides to adopt a riskier and more aggressive development.

12. B—Kt2
13. B—Kt2 Kt—B3
14. Kt—K5 O—O
15. P×P

Threatening 16 Kt×Ktch., B×Kt; 17 R—Q7, winning a piece.

15. Kt—Q4
16. KR—K1

The attempt to win a pawn by P×P may lead to trouble after Q×P; 17 Kt—Q7, Q—K6ch.; 18 Q—Q2, KR—Q1; 19 Kt—K5, Q×Qch.; 20 R×Q, Kt—K6; 21 B—B3, P—B3; 22 R—K1, P×Kt; 23 R×Kt, P×P; 24 P×P, P—K4.

16. P×P
17. P—KR4 P—B3

Now Black rids himself of the pressure and frees his pieces for action, though at the cost of a weak KP.

18. Kt—B3 Q—R4
19. P—R4

That White is already in difficulties is revealed by his having recourse to this awkward dedefence. The more natural looking P—R3 allows Black to sacrifice on his QR6. For example, 19 P—R3, P—B5; 20 B—R3, P—B4; 21 Kt(4)—Kt5, B×P; 22 P×B, Kt×QBP; 23 R—Q4 (R—Q7, B—B3; 24 R—K7, QR—Kt1), QR—Kt1; 24 Kt—K5, B—K5ch.; 25 Kt×B, Q×Pch.; 26 K—Q2, Kt×Ktch.; 27 K—Q1, R—Kt7.

19. B—B3
20. B—R3

Playing to avoid the loss of the exchange would allow Black a strong game after 20 P—Kt3, P—B5; or 20 Q—K2, B×P; 21 R—Q2 (or Q3), B—Kt6. White prefers to retain attacking chances at the cost of material and fixes on the weak KP as an objective.

20. P—B4
21. Kt(4)—Kt5 B×P
22. Q—K2 B×R
23. Q×Pch K—R1
24. R×B

Not 24 Q×Kt, Q—R8ch.; 25 K—Q2, QR—Q1; nor 24 Kt—K5, Q—R8ch.; 25 K—Q2, Q×Pch.; 26 K×B (K—Q3, Q×P Mate), Kt×P Mate, nor 24 Kt—B7ch., R×Kt; 25 Q×R, Q—R8ch.; mating in the same way. Now White threatens to recover material by Kt—B7 ch. as well as by capturing the bishop if the knight moves. Black, however, keeps the attack going with a brilliant sacrifice of the bishop.

(BLACK) KATETOV

(WHITE) SMYSLOV

Position before Black's 24th move.

(DIAGRAM 64)

24. Kt×QBP
25. Q×B

Not 25 Kt—B7ch., R×Kt; 26 Q×R, Kt×R; 27 Q×B, R—Q1; wins.

25. QR—K1
26. Q—Q7 Kt×R
27. Kt—B7ch. K—Kt1
28. B×P

He still cannot recover his material, for if 28 K×Kt, R—Q1; 29 Kt×R, R×Kt; and wins. Now he threatens to draw by Kt—R6ch.

28. Q—Kt3
29. Kt(3)—K5 Kt—K6
30. Kt—Q6

The White counter-attack now reaches its peak. Black cannot reply 30 . . ., R—Q1; because of the well-known mate by 31 Q—K6ch., K—R1; 32 Kt(5)—B7ch., K—Kt1; 33 Kt—R6 dis. ch., K—R1; 34 Q—Kt8ch., R×Q; 35 Kt (Q)—B7 Mate.

30. Kt×B
31. Kt×R Q—Kt6

Black is suddenly in difficulties. He is faced not only with the threat of a check on the dangerous diagonal by Q—Q5 but also with the threat of P—KKt4 and if the knight moves, Q×P Mate.

32. P—Kt4 Q—K6ch.
33. K—Kt1 Q×P
34. Q—K6ch. K—R1
35. P×Kt

Kt—B7ch., R×Kt; 36 Q×R, Q—K5ch.; allows Black a draw by perpetual check, for if 37 K—B1, Q—K8ch.; 38 K—B2, Kt—Q5ch.; and Black mates.

35. Q×Pch.

Forcing the queen off just in time and very nearly securing an end-game advantage. But some adroit manipulation of the White knight's brings them into co-ordination and holds the fort.

36. Q×Q R×Q
37. Kt—Q6 R—B8ch.
38. K—B2 R—KR8
39. Kt—B3 R—R6
40. Kt—B7ch. K—Kt1
41. Kt(7)—K5 R—Kt6
42. K—Q3 R—Kt7

Drawn.

Black can force a passed KKtP at the cost of his QBP. The balance on the Q side is then level, and two knights can hold rook and pawn on the other.

INDEX OF OPENINGS

(The numbers refer to the numbers of the games)

OPEN KP GAMES :

Giuoco Piano 3, 9
Evans Gambit 8
Scotch Game 22, 44
Ponziani Opening. 33
Ruy Lopez 5, 7, 14, 20, 21, 24, 29, 48
Petroff Defence. 16
King's Bishop's Opening 1, 4, 6
Falkbeer Counter Gambit 18
Centre Game 28

CLOSE KP GAMES :

Alekhine Defence 32, 41
French Defence 12, 50
Sicilian Defence 23, 27

QUEEN'S GAMBIT GAMES :

Queen's Gambit 2, 39
Pillsbury Attack 15, 19, 26, 34, 36, 38
Tarrasch Defence 25
Slav Defence 30
Irregular Queen's Gambit Declined 10

CLOSE Q-SIDE GAMES :

Nimzo-Indian Defence 35, 45, 46, 49
King's Indian Defence 42
Dutch Defence 47
Tchigorin Defence 17
Colle System 40
Irregular Queen's Pawn Game . . . 11, 13, 37, 43
Reti System 31